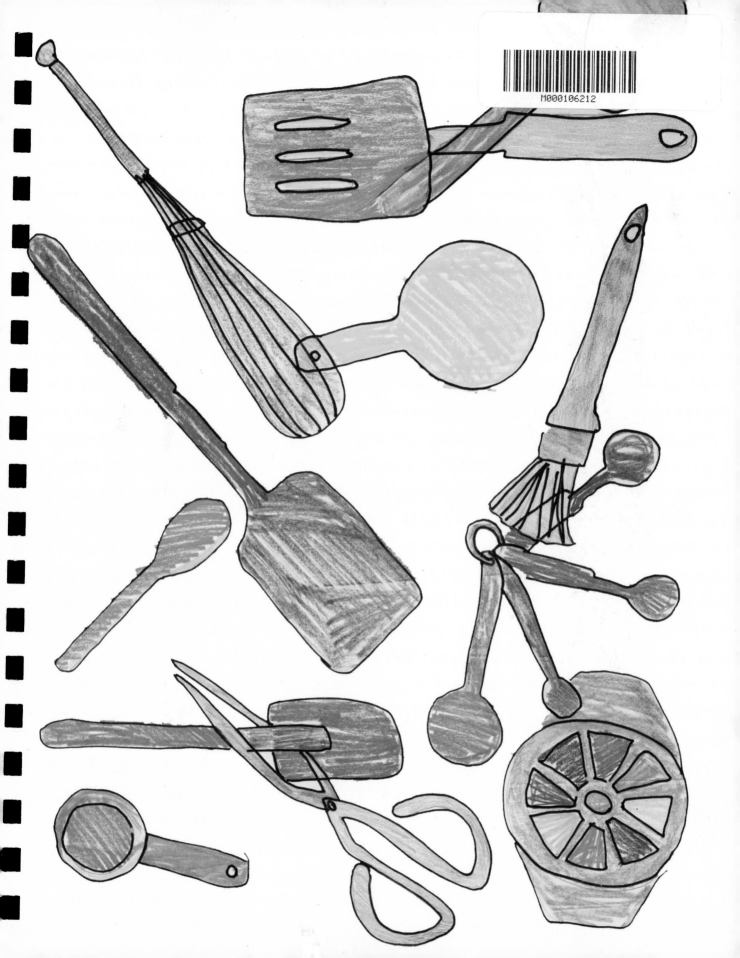

M000106212

THE

Cooking with Kids
COOKBOOK

Lynn Walters and Jane Stacey

with Gabrielle Gonzales

Foreword by
Cheryl Alters Jamison and Deborah Madison

University of New Mexico Press • *Albuquerque*

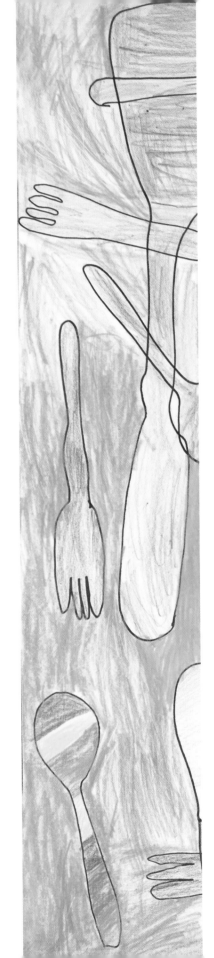

Contents

Salads

Main Dishes

Fruits and Sweets

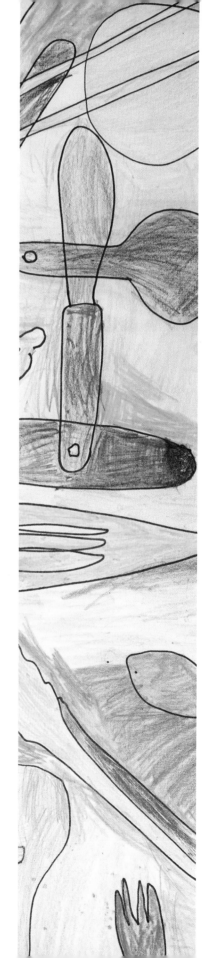

Foreword

You hold in your hands a recipe—many recipes, actually—for success in your family kitchen. Since 1995 Santa Fe's Cooking with Kids has educated and empowered thousands of schoolchildren to make healthy food choices through hands-on learning with fresh, affordable foods from diverse cultures. Kids who help plan, prepare, and cook meals are much more likely to enjoy a broad array of foods, many more than adults often imagine. In this cookbook, written for families to use together, and for older youth to explore on their own, the beloved New Mexico nonprofit organization shares its most enthusiastically kid-endorsed dishes. Included too are Cooking with Kids' time-tested tips for engaging children in the kitchen—and in the garden as well.

The challenge of feeding our children wholesome, truly good food has become a major topic of national conversation in recent years. Cooking with Kids founder Lynn Walters and program director Jane Stacey were among the activists who helped kick off the conversation, with their then-novel approach of involving kids, parents, chefs, teachers, principals, and school-cafeteria workers in improving what goes on the table and into kids' mouths. Some two decades after the organization's founding, more than 5,000 children are touched by the program each year. Cooking with Kids provides most of the funding, original curriculum, trained educators, home recipes in English and Spanish, and all related materials for guided lessons with healthy, fresh, and affordable foods. The organization's educators teach cooking classes during the school day to prekindergarten through sixth-grade students in partnership with teachers and family volunteers.

Both of us are proud to be associated with Cooking with Kids and to have seen firsthand the impact it has had on what kids will eat, both at school and at home. We have watched pint-sized participants taste a half-dozen varieties of late-summer, vine-ripened tomatoes from nearby farms, eyes wide and smiling mouths dribbling juice, as they discover the remarkable range of flavors.

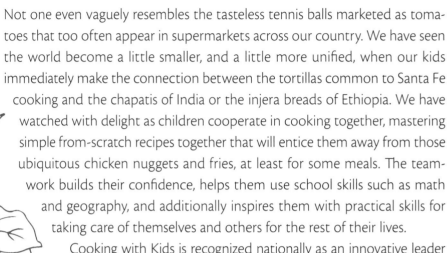

Not one even vaguely resembles the tasteless tennis balls marketed as tomatoes that too often appear in supermarkets across our country. We have seen the world become a little smaller, and a little more unified, when our kids immediately make the connection between the tortillas common to Santa Fe cooking and the chapatis of India or the injera breads of Ethiopia. We have watched with delight as children cooperate in cooking together, mastering simple from-scratch recipes together that will entice them away from those ubiquitous chicken nuggets and fries, at least for some meals. The teamwork builds their confidence, helps them use school skills such as math and geography, and additionally inspires them with practical skills for taking care of themselves and others for the rest of their lives.

Cooking with Kids is recognized nationally as an innovative leader in hands-on food and nutrition education. Chef Jamie Oliver's Food Revolution chose Cooking with Kids' Green and White Fettuccine with Tomato Basil Sauce and accompanying salad as one of the country's best school lunches. Southwest Lentils, a recipe created by a fifth-grade Cooking with Kids class, was selected as a winner in First Lady Michelle Obama's Recipes for Healthy Kids competition. The International Association of Culinary Professionals named Cooking with Kids as its exemplary culinary nonprofit organization of 2013. Additionally, the organization has been honored with a national Innovation in Prevention Award by the US Department of Health and Human Services for its efforts in promoting healthy lifestyles.

Childhood experiences with food—the joy of growing it, preparing it, and then sharing it at the table with family and friends—were among the most formative life events for both of us. They remain among our most treasured memories and delights today. We are sure this book can help share the joy of cooking with kids in your life, while expanding the culinary horizons of adults and children alike in nurturing and nutritious ways. Dig in today.

Cheryl Alters Jamison and Deborah Madison

Introduction

"This Is Good Because We Made It!"

The heart of Cooking with Kids is hands-on learning with foods inspired by the diverse cuisines of the world. In our hurry-up lives it can be a challenge to know when and how to invite children into the kitchen and the garden. The intention for this book, which grew out of Cooking with Kids' work with thousands of schoolchildren, is to provide a real-world guide for engaging children in garden-to-table experiences. Cooking with children reminds us that working together to nourish ourselves is a joy—sometimes messy, but almost always great fun!

We all eat—every day if we're lucky. Food itself tells the stories of people, and many treasure memories of a favorite grandmothers' dish, perhaps made with aromatic herbs from the garden or juicy, ripe fruit from a neighbor's tree. Not so long ago, growing our own food was part of the process of getting it on the table, and culinary traditions evolved based on the plants and animals that thrived in distinct climatic conditions. Revealing vast differences and sometimes surprising similarities, the varied cuisines of the world offer an opportunity to connect us all through the foods that we depend upon and share. We hope that you delight in your family food traditions and are inspired to create new ones by cooking these tried and true recipes and planting a few seeds with your children.

A Note from a Cooking with Kids Educator

As an AmeriCorps volunteer in Santa Fe, New Mexico, I had very little idea of what I would be doing when I began working with Cooking with Kids. I knew that the organization was a nonprofit dedicated to teaching elementary school children about healthy eating and cooking. As the first months passed, it began to dawn on me how incredibly fortunate I was, even though I had never worked so hard in my life. And over the course of that year, I experienced my definition of magic.

In the beginning of the school year, kindergarteners knew nothing about how melons grew. A few months later, they eagerly told me the definition of a root vegetable, and they could even give examples! I witnessed older students who struggled with traditional public-school education succeed in an experiential learning environment. It was moving to see third graders recognize their own ability to cook, to use a knife safely and skillfully, and to learn the difference between "chop" and "mince." Kids cooked and ate purple potatoes, homemade egg noodles, and pizza made from scratch. Fifth graders, who insisted they never ate tomatoes or onions, scarfed down Vegetable Paella (page 64) and Red Lentils (page 70). I saw how these hands-on experiences inspired children to eat fresh fruits and vegetables.

My dream was to work at a nonprofit and make a difference in its community. I'm so proud that I helped make that magic happen, drawing on my strength and energy to teach cooking classes. I know that Cooking with Kids makes an immense impact in the community, and I hope it can continue to do so, paving the way for future generations of students and adults to live in a happy and healthy world.

Gabrielle Gonzales

A Note from the Author: In the Garden

When I was eight, my father rented a small field from a nearby farmer for two summers. I helped him tend the tall green corn that we grew there. I remember helping to prop up the corn plants after one particularly strong summer storm that seemed like it must have been (but wasn't) a hurricane. The mud was warm and wonderfully squishy between my toes, but every once in a while a stickery weed would interrupt my plant-tending reverie. In my child-mind, these were the most peaceful and beautiful times with my dad.

That cornfield experience was the only real gardening of my childhood, with the exceptions of my mother's occasional forays into growing radishes and tomatoes and my grandmother's lemon tree and gladiolus. That wondrous childhood cornfield memory lay dormant until early adulthood, when it blossomed into a full-blown garden wonder. Every summer, I watched with pleasure as my children ran through our cornfield, laughing, with hair flying and hands rustling long green, and sometimes purple, corn leaves. With that, I encourage you to venture into the world of edible plants with your children.

Lynn Walters

From the Garden to the Table—Together

At first, cooking or gardening side by side with little ones may take more time than doing it yourself, and it may create a bit of a mess. However, there is no replacement for hands-on learning. You will be surprised at how competent and confident children are in the kitchen, how much they love to dig in the dirt when given the chance, how they even like to help clean up.

Cooking and gardening with children is most enjoyable when everyone has something to do. As with any experiment, it is important to pay attention, to practice patience, and to be curious about the outcome. Safety and respect are also part of the equation. Be watchful, but try not to hover. Being outside with plants or in the kitchen with food is a pleasure when each person has a role and is valued for their contribution—everyone works best with praise and encouragement. Most importantly, relax and have fun!

Tried and True Guidelines for Success in the Kitchen or in the Garden

Encourage and allow kids to do as much as possible. When you are about to take the next step in a recipe, pause and ask yourself, "Could a child be doing this?"

Simple, clear, and specific directions are more effective than long-winded explanations for many kids. Let them in on the action right away!

With guidance, using kitchen knives and garden implements can be safe for children, and they will feel proud of using real tools.

Include everyone in a comfortable way: In the kitchen, sometimes a shy child might only want to tear up herbs, while another wants to do all of the measuring and mixing, and another is clear about only wanting to read the recipe. In the garden, some children will dig right in, but others might be happiest counting seeds.

Before You Begin

Wash hands.

Assemble ingredients and cookware.

Wash all produce: vegetables, fruits, and herbs.

Read the recipe all the way through.

Cooking with Kids: The Basics

Rolling dough (pizza/flatbread/tortillas) is really fun for everyone.

Tearing lettuces and greens for salad is easy, and it's a great way to demonstrate being gentle.

Making fruit salads is a great way to start learning to cut with a knife.

Include cleanup as part of the job—kids love water!

Keep little ones busy with washing vegetables, using a brush and a half-filled tub of water.

Instead of mincing with a knife, little kids can tear leafy herbs into tiny pieces. Children of any age can peel garlic or shell peas.

Butter knives work quite well to cut zucchini, yellow squash, and cucumbers.

Knife Skills

Be a good role model by emphasizing safety, respect, and responsibility.

Stand while you cut.

Always use a knife on a cutting board. To keep the cutting board from slipping, place it on a damp towel.

Make round foods flat on one side by cutting them in half before slicing or chopping them.

Never put knives in a sink or a dishpan.

Do not allow children to carry or wash knives.

Adults: carry a knife at your side, with the tip of the knife pointing toward the floor.

How to Hold a Knife

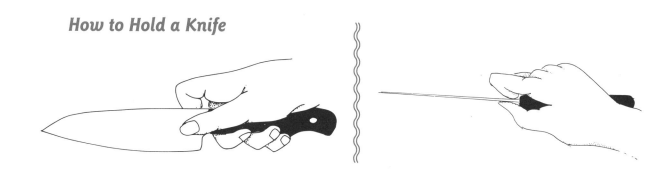

For chopping and mincing, hold the knife with both hands on top of the blade.

Soups and Small Plates

Soups and Small Plates

Sometimes little appetites don't demand a big meal—sometimes everyone just wants to eat a little something to feel satisfied. Grown-ups like to eat this way, so why wouldn't kids? These small plates can serve either as light meals or appetizers, and they're also an easy way to try out something new.

Soups are a great way to use recipes as a starting point, but then to go beyond the recipe by varying the vegetables and herbs. After cooking together, include children in deciding how to serve the soup, and let them in on the fun of garnishing with herbs or edible flower petals. Little kids may enjoy eating from tiny soup cups or teacups. Shallow pasta dishes are another option, as they allow the soup to cool more quickly than traditional soup bowls. Serve soups with flatbread or breadsticks and sweet butter.

The small plates in this chapter include a variety of vegetables prepared using different methods—shredded, roasted, mashed, or made into little cakes and sautéed. They are good on their own or can be paired with other dishes.

Minestrone

What Kids Can Do

Peel carrots and garlic

Wash vegetables

Tear kale and herbs

Cooks' Notes

❀ Serve with Breadsticks (page 112) and Pesto (page 5) as a garnish or for dipping.

❀ Use the bottom of a can to smash each garlic clove and the skins will slip off very easily.

❀ Older children appreciate the responsibility of stirring food at the stove. For little ones, bring the cooking pot to the table, set it on a trivet, and let them take turns stirring.

Minestrone is a favorite of many children we know, especially when garnished generously with Parmesan cheese and served with breadsticks for dunking. This quick version uses canned beans, but if you have time, cook dry beans with plenty of water—they will warm your kitchen and cost a lot less too.

Serves 4 to 6

2 tablespoons olive oil

½ medium onion, chopped

2 garlic cloves, chopped

1 celery stalk, chopped

1 carrot, cut into ¼-inch pieces

¼ teaspoon dried thyme

1 cup crushed tomatoes

2 cups broth, chicken or vegetable

2 cups water

1 bay leaf

⅛ teaspoon dried oregano

¾ teaspoon salt

¼ teaspoon freshly ground black pepper

1 zucchini, quartered lengthwise and thinly sliced

1 (15-ounce) can white beans or ½ cup dry white beans (navy or cannellini), cooked

1 cup fresh or frozen Italian green beans

¾ cup chopped kale

2 tablespoons chopped parsley

2 teaspoons chopped fresh basil or 1 teaspoon dried basil

¾ cup small whole wheat pasta, cooked

Shredded Parmesan cheese

1 Heat the olive oil in a large pot. Add the onion and garlic and sauté for 3 to 5 minutes over medium-high heat until softened. Add the celery and carrots. Cook for 5 to 7 minutes, stirring often.

2 Stir in the crushed tomatoes. Add the broth, water, bay leaf, oregano, thyme, salt, and pepper. Increase the heat to high and bring to a boil. Stir in the zucchini, white beans, and green beans.

3 When the soup returns to boiling, reduce the heat to medium and simmer, partially covered, for about 15 minutes, until all the vegetables are tender. Add the chopped kale and parsley, and cook for several minutes more, until the greens are wilted.

4 Just before serving, sprinkle in the chopped basil.

5 Spoon pasta into the bottom of each soup bowl. Ladle hot soup over the pasta and top with shredded Parmesan cheese.

Let's Grow Beans!

Romano beans are a classic Italian flat green bean with a hearty flavor. They remain tender, even when the beans grow large. Romano beans are available in both bush and pole types. Bush bean plants grow to about 3 feet high, while pole beans grow to about 6 feet.

Beans are warm-weather plants, so plant bean seeds in late spring, around the date of the last spring frost. Follow the rule of planting seeds about 3 times as deep as the size of the seed. Plant bean seeds 1 inch deep and about 6 inches apart.

Pole beans can be trained to create a living playhouse.

1 Lay 7 wooden poles (at least 8 feet tall) on the ground and tie them together about 18 inches from the top. With some help, stand them up and then separate the poles, spacing them evenly, to create a circle with a 4- to 5-foot diameter. Leave a space for an opening about 2 feet wide, facing east, if possible, so that the morning sun will warm the cozy space.

2 Plant 2 to 3 seeds on either side of each pole, with additional seeds spaced about 6 inches apart between the poles.

3 Water the seeds every day until the beans sprout. Then water once or twice a week, as needed, while the bean plants are growing.

4 Tie strings around the outside of the playhouse for the bean tendrils to grab as the plants climb.

Pesto

The heat of late summer is the time to make fresh basil pesto. Although it is faster to make pesto in a food processor, children have a great time mashing and grinding using the mortar and pestle!

Makes about 1 cup

2 garlic cloves

¼ teaspoon salt

¼ cup pine nuts or walnuts

3 cups fresh basil leaves

⅓ cup grated Parmesan or Romano cheese

½ cup olive oil

1 Using a mortar and pestle, smash the garlic and nuts until they are well crushed.

2 Tear the basil leaves into pieces, add them a handful at a time, and work the mixture into a fine paste. Stir in the cheese and olive oil.

What Kids Can Do

Peel garlic

Wash basil

Grind all the ingredients using the mortar and pestle

Grate cheese (watch those knuckles)

Cooks' Notes

For best results, use the pesto immediately. If storing in the refrigerator, seal the top with plastic wrap to keep the pesto from turning brown. Some people like to freeze pesto in ice-cube trays, to pull out as needed.

Pesto can also be made without cheese or without any nuts at all.

Southwest Lentils
(or Sweeney Cougar Power Lentils)

What Kids Can Do

Wash vegetables

Peel garlic

Measure ingredients

Dice tomatoes

Tear cilantro

Cooks' Note

✂ Serve with a quesadilla for a satisfying lunch.

Lentils may seem surprising as a child-friendly food, but we have found them to be versatile and widely enjoyed. This prize-winning recipe was developed by fifth-grade students at Sweeney Elementary School in Santa Fe.

Serves 6 as a side dish

1 cup brown or green lentils

3 cups water

2 teaspoons olive oil

¼ cup chopped onion

2 garlic cloves, minced

1 teaspoon ground cumin

1½ teaspoons ground mild red chile
or 1 teaspoon chili powder

⅔ cup diced tomatoes

½ teaspoon salt

¼ cup chopped cilantro

1 Combine the lentils and water in a saucepan. Bring to a boil over high heat, then skim off and discard any foam that appears. Reduce the heat to medium and cook the lentils until tender, partially covered, for about an hour. If needed, add more water.

2 Heat the oil in a large pot. Add the onion and garlic and sauté for 2 to 3 minutes, until softened. Stir in the cumin and the ground red chile or chili powder. Add the cooked lentils with their juice, the tomatoes, and the salt. Bring the mixture to a boil, reduce the heat to low, and simmer, uncovered, for about 10 minutes.

3 Just before serving, stir in the chopped cilantro or use it as a garnish for the lentils.

Asian Noodles

You might be surprised how easy these homemade noodles are to make! No fancy equipment is needed—just a few ingredients and a rolling pin. Kids can measure, mix, and learn to separate eggs! Crack an egg into your child's hand held over a bowl. Watch the egg white drip through their fingers—the yolk will be left in their hand, and they can gently place it into another bowl.

Serves 4 to 6

What Kids Can Do

Measure ingredients

Separate eggs

Mix and roll out dough

Cooks' Notes

- Toast the sesame seeds in a small skillet over medium-high heat, stirring constantly until lightly browned. Put the toasted seeds into a small bowl to cool.

- One way to cut carrots into matchsticks: Cut the carrots in half. Then cut each half lengthwise and lay the flat side down on the cutting board. Using a sharp knife, slice at a deep angle to form thin half-moon-shaped slices. Then cut each thin slice into 3 or 4 long, thin pieces, about the size and shape of a wooden match.

- Experiment with using different types of greens, such as Swiss chard, spinach, or tatsoi.

- Make it a heartier dish by adding cubes of tofu or cooked chicken.

Egg Noodles

> **3 egg yolks**
>
> **¾ cup water**
>
> **3 cups unbleached white flour**
>
> **½ teaspoon salt**

Broth and Vegetables

> **6 cups broth, chicken or vegetable**
>
> **2 tablespoons soy sauce**
>
> **½ teaspoon peeled and minced fresh ginger**
>
> **2 carrots, peeled and cut into matchsticks**
>
> **1½ cups bok choy or Chinese cabbage, chopped**
>
> **2 green onions, thinly sliced**

Garnishes

> **2 tablespoons sesame seeds, toasted**
>
> **2 tablespoons chopped cilantro**

1 Make the noodles: In a bowl, mix together the flour and salt. In another bowl, whisk together the egg yolks and water, then add to the dry mixture and stir until a dough forms. On a clean, lightly floured work surface, knead the dough for 3 minutes, until it is smooth.

2 Cover the dough with a clean cloth and let it rest for 15 to 20 minutes. Cut the dough into 8 equal pieces. Use a rolling pin to roll each piece of dough into a rectangular shape about 3 inches wide, 12 inches long, and about ⅛ inch thick. Dust the strips of dough with flour to keep them from sticking. Cut the dough crosswise into strips about ½ inch wide and 3 inches long. Transfer the noodles to several cookie sheets, keeping the noodles separate from each other.

3 Make the broth: Combine the broth, soy sauce, and ginger in a saucepan and bring to a boil over high heat. Add the carrots and bok choy, reduce the heat, and cook for 2 to 3 minutes. Remove from the heat, add the green onions, and cover.

4 While the broth is heating, cook the noodles: Bring a large pot of water to a boil over high heat. Add the egg noodles and cook until tender, about 4 minutes. Drain the noodles in a colander and rinse with cool water to stop them from cooking.

5 Ladle the hot broth over the noodles and garnish with toasted sesame seeds and cilantro.

Making Vegetable Stock

Beans and lentils give soups a hearty, rich flavor. But many soups will benefit from using homemade or canned stock, which will add a depth of flavor. Simple homemade vegetable broth can be made easily. Fill a large pot half full of water, then add chopped onion, carrots, celery, a few favorite herbs, and a bay leaf. Bring to a boil, then reduce the heat and simmer for an hour or two. Strain out the cooked vegetables, and that's it!

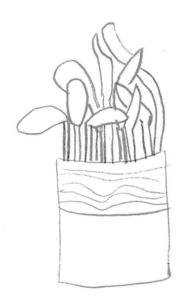

Potato Pancakes

What Kids Can Do

Scrub and peel potatoes

Grate potatoes
(watch those knuckles)

Crack eggs

Measure flour

Mix ingredients

Cooks' Notes

✄ Serve hot with Homemade Applesauce (page 135) and sour cream.

✄ Substitute 1 cup peeled and grated parsnip or sweet potato for 1 cup of the potatoes.

✄ To protect little hands from scrapes, cover the sides of the grater that aren't being used with duct tape.

Baking potatoes, often called russet or Idaho potatoes, make crisp and tender potato pancakes. Kids will enjoy cracking the eggs and grating little mountains of potatoes, but watch their little knuckles.

Serves 4 to 6

3 baking potatoes (about 4½ cups grated potatoes)

1 green onion, thinly sliced

2 eggs, beaten

¾ teaspoon salt

¼ cup whole wheat or white flour

¼ teaspoon freshly ground black pepper

Vegetable oil for cooking

1 cup sour cream

1 Peel the potatoes. Use the side of the grater with the largest holes to grate potatoes directly into a bowl of cold water, which keeps them from turning brown. Transfer the grated potatoes into a colander. Press the potatoes to squeeze out as much liquid as possible.

2 In a large bowl, mix together the eggs, salt, and pepper. Add the flour, whisking to combine. Stir in the grated potatoes and sliced green onions and mix well.

3 Heat 3 tablespoons of oil in a skillet over high heat. Spoon about 2 tablespoons of the potato mixture to form each potato pancake. Flatten the pancakes with a spatula and cook for 4 to 5 minutes on each side, until they are dark golden brown and cooked through. Add more oil as needed and continue to cook the pancakes.

How Many Potatoes?

Draw 3 yellow potatoes.

Draw 2 purple potatoes.

Draw 5 pink potatoes.

Count the potatoes. How many are there?

Zucchini Cakes

What Kids Can Do

Grate zucchini
(watch those knuckles)

Crack eggs

Mix ingredients

Cooks' Notes

✂ Serve with Tomato Cucumber Salad (page 36).

✂ Use shredded cheddar or mozzarella instead of feta cheese.

The process of making these zucchini cakes is similar to making potato pancakes. Mix up the batter, get the skillet on the stove, and you're ready to eat.

Serves 4 to 6

3 medium zucchini	½ teaspoon salt
2 green onions, thinly sliced	2 eggs, beaten
2 tablespoons minced parsley	
1 teaspoon dried oregano	
⅛ teaspoon freshly ground black pepper	
3 tablespoons flour	
½ cup crumbled feta cheese (optional)	
Vegetable oil for cooking	

1 Use the side of the grater with the largest holes to grate the zucchini into a colander. Place the colander in a bowl, sprinkle the zucchini with salt, and let it sit for 15 minutes. Squeeze as much liquid out of the grated zucchini as possible by pressing it against the colander.

2 Put the grated zucchini into a large bowl. Add the onion, eggs, parsley, oregano, pepper, flour, and feta cheese (if using). Stir until just combined.

3 Heat 2 tablespoons of oil in a skillet over medium-high heat. Form heaping spoonfuls of the zucchini mixture into small patties and place in the skillet. Cook for 3 to 4 minutes on each side, until the patties are dark golden brown on both sides. Add more vegetable oil, as needed, and continue to cook the patties.

Hummus—Three Ways

Kids love to mash, mash, mash—a good reason not to use a food processor! Spread hummus on homemade flatbread, crackers, pita chips, or bread—or use it as a dip with carrots, celery, bell pepper, snap peas, or another favorite vegetable.

Traditional Hummus

1 (15-ounce) can garbanzo beans, drained and rinsed, or ½ cup dry garbanzo beans, cooked

1 garlic clove, minced

2 tablespoons tahini

2 tablespoons olive oil

2 tablespoons freshly squeezed lemon juice

½ teaspoon ground cumin

¼ teaspoon salt

1 In a bowl, use a potato masher to mash the garbanzo beans until they are almost smooth.

2 Stir in the remaining ingredients and mix until well combined.

What Kids Can Do

Scrub sweet potatoes

Mash garbanzo beans

Measure ingredients

Peel garlic

Squeeze lemons

Mix ingredients

Cooks' Note

A food processor is a quick and easy way to blend all the ingredients together.

Did You Know?

Tahini is a paste made from raw or toasted sesame seeds that has been used in Middle Eastern cooking for centuries. It can be purchased in natural-food stores or specialty grocery stores.

Hummus is the Arabic word for garbanzo bean, or chickpea, the main ingredient of the original dip.

Spinach Hummus

1 cup fresh spinach leaves

1 (15-ounce) can garbanzo beans, drained and rinsed, or ½ cup dry garbanzo beans, cooked

2 tablespoons sesame tahini

1 garlic clove, minced

2 tablespoons olive oil

2 tablespoons freshly squeezed lemon juice

¼ teaspoon salt

1 Wash the spinach leaves and remove the stems. Finely chop the spinach and set aside.

2 In a bowl, use a potato masher to completely mash the garbanzo beans. Add the spinach, stir in the remaining ingredients, and mix until well combined.

Sweet Potato Hummus

2 medium sweet potatoes

1 (15-ounce) can garbanzo beans, drained and rinsed,
  or ½ cup dry garbanzo beans, cooked

2 tablespoons sesame tahini (optional)

¼ cup freshly squeezed lemon juice

¼ cup olive oil

2 garlic cloves, minced

1 teaspoon ground cumin

¾ teaspoon salt

¼ teaspoon freshly ground black pepper

1   Preheat oven to 400 degrees F. Use a fork or a paring knife to poke a few holes in the sweet potatoes and place on a baking sheet. Bake until tender, about an hour.

2   Let the sweet potatoes cool until comfortable to handle. Break the sweet potatoes in half and use a spoon to scoop out the flesh. Discard the skin.

3   Use a potato masher to completely mash the garbanzo beans. Add the sweet potatoes and continue to mash until smooth. Add the remaining ingredients and mix until well combined. If the mixture seems too thick, stir in a tablespoon of water at a time until the consistency seems right.

Roasted Root Vegetables

What Kids Can Do

Scrub vegetables

Peel carrots and parsnips

Rub vegetables
with oil

Cooks' Notes

❦ Instead of beets, use turnips or rutabagas in this recipe.

❦ As an addition, cook fresh beet or turnip greens to serve with the roasted vegetables: steam or sauté, then serve with a little butter and salt.

Roasting brings out the sweetness and deepens the flavors of root vegetables. Experiment with different combinations of spices and oils, or try roasting them right alongside a chicken.

Serves 4 to 6

2 carrots

2 beets

2 potatoes

2 parsnips

1 onion

5 fresh sage leaves (optional)

3 tablespoons olive oil

½ teaspoon salt

¼ teaspoon freshly ground black pepper

1 Preheat the oven to 425 degrees F.

2 Peel the carrots, parsnips, and beets. Cut the vegetables into 1-inch wedges and put them into a shallow baking pan, spreading them to form a single even layer. Scrub the potatoes and cut them into eighths. Add the potatoes to the pan. Cut the onion in half, then into ¼-inch-thick slices, and add to the pan.

3 Drizzle the olive oil over the vegetables and add the sage leaves (if using). Sprinkle with salt and pepper. Toss together so that the oil coats them evenly. Bake for 30 to 40 minutes, or until the vegetables are tender and lightly browned.

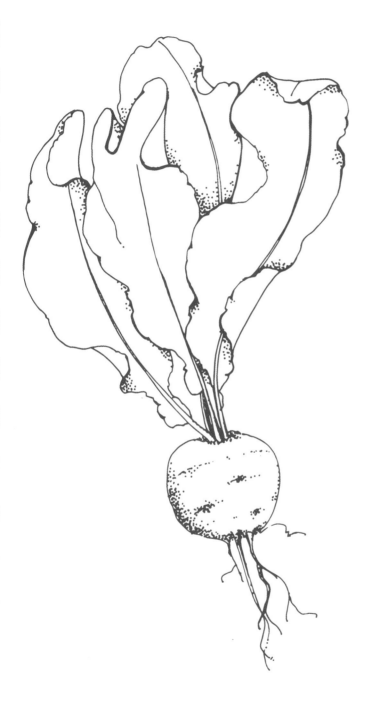

Let's Grow Carrots and Beets!

Carrots and beets keep their colors hidden underground until they are ready to harvest, while we see only the pretty green leaves above ground. Both of these root vegetables can be planted in the spring to be harvested in summer. A second planting can be made midsummer for a fall harvest. Carrot seeds are very tiny, so planting requires extra care.

1   Plant seeds about an inch apart.

2   Plant carrot seeds ¼ inch deep and beet seeds ½ inch deep.

3   When the plants are 3 inches tall, thin them to about 3 inches apart. The young plants are very tasty and can be used in salads.

4   Later, when the "shoulders" of the carrots and beets start to show, it will be time to harvest the roots.

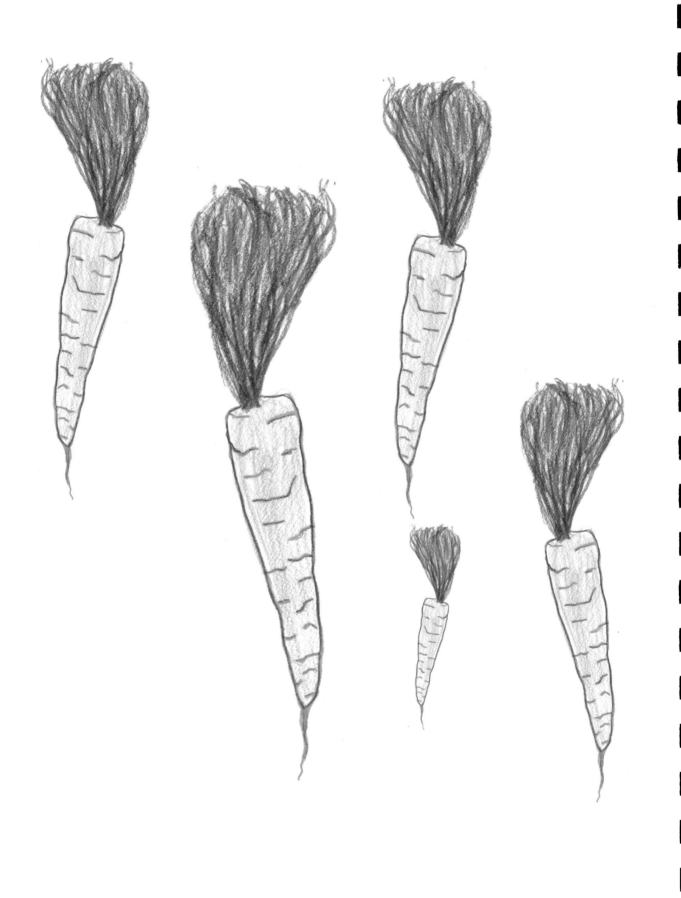

Salads

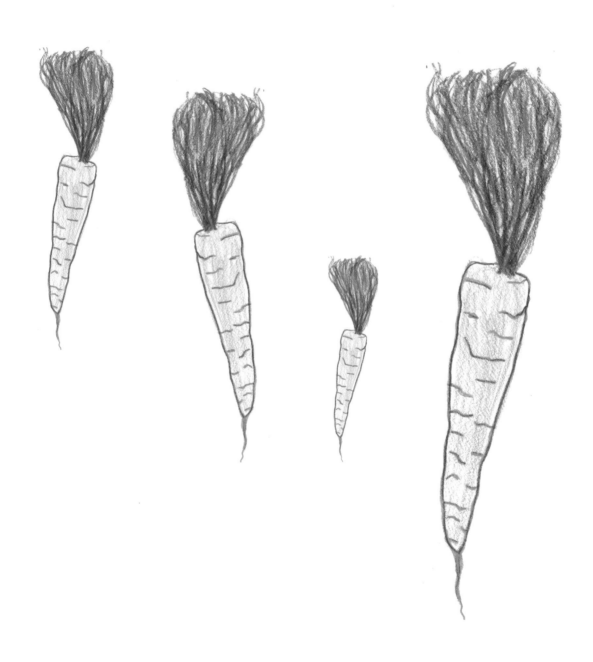

Salads

Crunchy greens with zingy dressings delight children more than you might imagine. After making a salad together, kids in our school program often ask for seconds! If you model how to *gently* handle and tear lettuce and explain that being gentle is important so that the lettuce doesn't bruise and lose its crunch, they'll follow suit.

Salads can be served in many ways. One way is to offer salad ingredients in separate bowls at the table.

And then there are dressings. Creamy dressings are alluring, vinaigrettes bring out the sweetness of fresh greens, and sometimes no dressing at all works best. One child may like to eat their salad plain and another may always want their favorite dressing. The tangy dressings in this chapter are easy to put together and go well with many vegetables.

Sometimes greens may be especially muddy, and they will require repeated soaking and draining to remove all of the dirt. When the greens are clean and drained, either dry them using a salad spinner or lay out the leaves on a clean dish towel and roll them up loosely, letting the towel absorb the water for 5 to 10 minutes. Use washed salad greens right away or store for a day or two in the vegetable drawer of your refrigerator.

Tricolor Salad with Balsamic Vinaigrette or Lemony Dressing

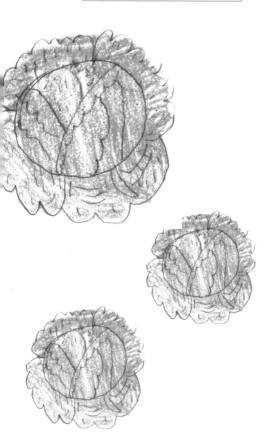

What Kids Can Do

Wash and tear lettuce

Peel and slice or grate carrots

Tear cabbage

Measure and whisk dressing

This colorful salad is a favorite. Most children—and many adults—appreciate a good crunch. The white stems of Romaine lettuce, the carrots, and the cabbage all have crisp textures and sweet flavors. Drizzle with either Balsamic Vinaigrette or Lemony Dressing (recipes follow).

Serves 4 to 6

Salad

1 small head Romaine lettuce   ⅛ head of red cabbage

1 carrot, peeled

1 Gently tear the lettuce into 2-inch pieces and put it into a serving bowl. Tear or cut the red cabbage into bite-sized pieces and add them to the lettuce.

2 Using the side of a grater with the largest holes, grate the carrot. Add the grated carrot to the serving bowl.

3 Just before serving, pour the dressing over the salad and toss until the salad is evenly coated.

Balsamic Vinaigrette

2 tablespoons balsamic vinegar

½ teaspoon Dijon mustard

¼ teaspoon salt

⅛ teaspoon freshly ground black pepper

1 tablespoon olive oil

⅓ cup sunflower or other vegetable oil

Balsamic Vinaigrette (continued)

1 In a small bowl, whisk together the vinegar, mustard, salt, and pepper.

2 Add the oils in a slow, steady stream, whisking constantly until the mixture is well combined.

Lemony Dressing

2 tablespoons freshly squeezed lemon juice

1 teaspoon Dijon mustard

¼ teaspoon salt

⅛ teaspoon freshly ground black pepper

¼ teaspoon sugar

1 tablespoon olive oil

⅓ cup sunflower or other vegetable oil

1 In a small bowl, whisk together the lemon juice, mustard, salt, pepper, and sugar.

2 Add the oils in a slow, steady stream, whisking constantly until the mixture is well combined.

Salad Greens with Creamy Lime Dressing

What Kids Can Do

Wash and tear lettuce

Peel and slice cucumber

Measure and whisk dressing

You don't really need a recipe to make a salad! Experiment by using a combination of sweet and tender butter lettuce with red leaf or oakleaf lettuce, and remind everyone to tear the lettuce gently so that it doesn't bruise. Cucumbers are soft enough for kids to slice using a butter knife.

Serves 4 to 6

> **1 to 2 small heads of leaf lettuce (about 7 cups)**
> **1 head curly endive**
> **1 cucumber, peeled and sliced**
> **5 radishes, thinly sliced**

1 Gently tear the lettuce and endive into 2-inch pieces and put into a serving bowl. Add the cucumber and radishes.

2 Just before serving, pour the dressing over the salad and toss until the salad is evenly coated. Serve immediately.

Creamy Lime Dressing

Kids sometimes call this dressing "ranch." It is great on greens, and it also makes a lovely sauce for grilled salmon.

½ teaspoon grated lime zest (the green part of the skin)

1 tablespoon fresh lime juice

2 tablespoons water

½ cup sour cream

⅛ teaspoon paprika

½ teaspoon sugar

¼ teaspoon salt

1 Wash the lime and grate the lime zest. Squeeze enough lime juice to equal 1 tablespoon. In a small bowl, combine the lime juice, water, and lime zest.

2 In a separate bowl, stir together the sour cream, paprika, sugar, and salt.

3 Whisk the lime juice mixture into the sour cream mixture until it is smooth.

Did You Know?

Paprika is made from dried sweet red peppers. It adds a sweet and earthy flavor.

Lettuces first grew as wild plants in Europe, Asia, and North Africa. These refreshing vegetables have been grown for almost 5,000 years.

Let's Grow Greens!

Salad greens like cool weather best, so spring and fall are generally peak planting times. Mixed lettuce seeds are now readily available and can be grown outside or even in a window box. Just follow the directions on the seed packet! Plant into good garden soil, and keep well watered. If you live in a hot climate, choose a spot that has some shade during part of the day.

Try growing a variety of Boston butter, oak-leaf, Black-Seeded Simpson, and Buttercrunch lettuce. And, while these leafy greens like cool weather, there are some varieties that will withstand summer heat as long as they get consistent water. If your family eats lots of salads, try succession planting—start a small new patch every month or two for a continuous supply.

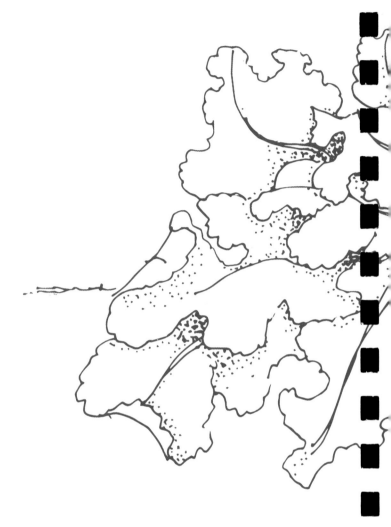

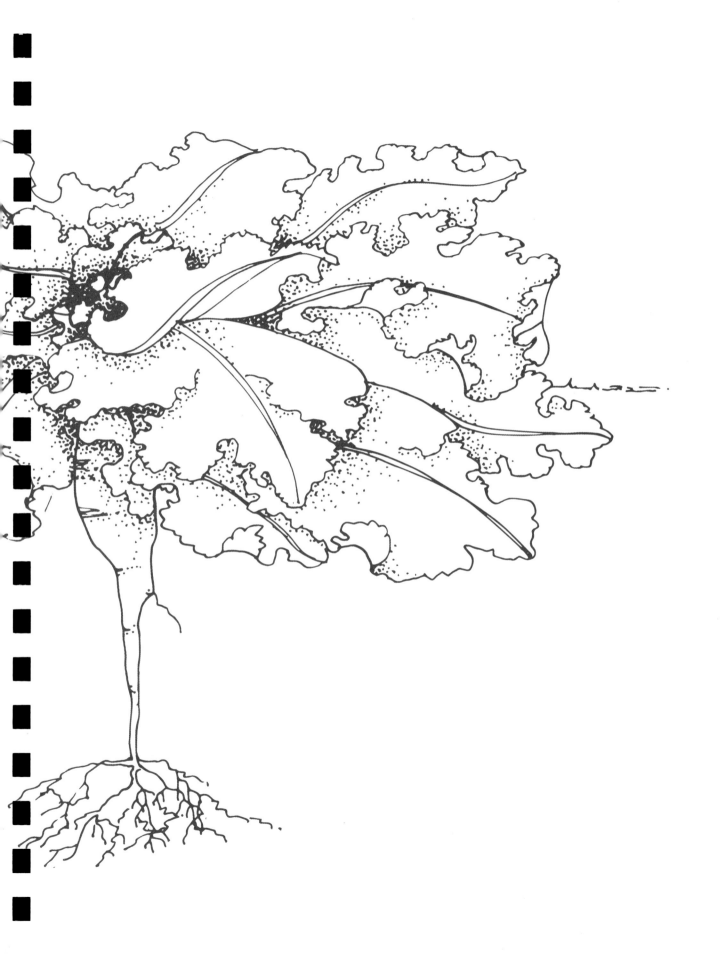

Spinach Salad with Citrus Vinaigrette

What Kids Can Do

Wash and tear spinach

Peel and cut cucumber

Squeeze citrus juice

Did You Know?

Spinach is a cool-weather crop that grows sweeter as the weather turns cold.

Spinach is the star of this favorite spring salad. Cucumber and fennel add a sweet crunch.

Serves 4 to 6

Spinach Salad

4 cups baby spinach (about 6 ounces)

1 head Boston lettuce or ½ head Romaine lettuce

2 cucumbers

½ fennel bulb

1 Gently tear the spinach and lettuce into 2-inch pieces and put into large bowl.

2 Peel the cucumber. Cut it lengthwise, then crossways into thin slices.

3 Cut the fennel bulb lengthwise, remove the core, then slice very thin. Add the cucumber and fennel to the greens.

4 Just before serving, pour the dressing over the salad and toss until the salad is evenly coated.

Citrus Vinaigrette

Kids love to squeeze citrus juice using a simple hand juicer. They often plead to drink the tangy leftover lemon or lime juice, no matter how sour!

2 tablespoons fresh orange juice

1 tablespoon fresh lime juice

¼ teaspoon salt

⅛ teaspoon freshly ground black pepper

¼ cup sunflower or other vegetable oil

Pinch ground red chile (optional)

1 tablespoon sesame seeds

1 In a bowl, whisk together the orange juice, lime juice, salt, pepper, and red chile (if using). Add the oil in a slow, steady stream, whisking constantly until the mixture is well combined.

2 Toast the sesame seeds in a small skillet over medium-high heat, stirring constantly until lightly browned. Add the toasted seeds to the dressing.

Let's Grow Spinach!

1 Plant spinach seeds in the fall or spring, ½ inch deep and 2 inches apart, in rows spaced at least 8 inches apart.

2 Water consistently until the seeds sprout.

3 As the plants grow, thin the little plants— the tender young spinach thinnings are sweet and tasty to eat too—so that the neighboring plants barely touch.

4 Keep watering twice a week. As the spinach grows, you can pick the largest outside leaves individually. The whole plant will generally be ready to harvest 40 to 50 days after the seeds sprout.

Draw your favorite salad in a bowl. Then, write about how to make your salad.

Summer Lentil Salad

What Kids Can Do

Measure lentils and
salt and pepper

Chop chives

Mix ingredients

This salad came from an adventure that Jane's daughter, Eliza, had when working on a farm in France, outside of Paris. It is pure simplicity, made with lentils, olive oil, salt, pepper, and chives. Serve it for lunch with hard-boiled eggs, olives, baguettes, and juicy tomatoes from the garden.

Makes 4 cups

> 1¼ cups French lentils
>
> 3½ cups water
>
> ¼ cup olive oil
>
> ⅓ cup chopped fresh chives
>
> ½ teaspoon salt
>
> ¼ teaspoon freshly ground black pepper
>
> 2 to 3 sun-dried tomato halves, chopped

1 Cook the lentils: In a medium pot, combine the water and lentils and bring to a boil. Reduce the heat to low and simmer, partially covered, until tender but not mushy, about 25 minutes. Drain and rinse thoroughly.

2 Transfer the lentils to a bowl and add the remaining ingredients, mixing until well combined. Serve at room temperature.

Panzanella

This dish is made for helpers! Tearing bread and basil leaves are just the right jobs for little hands. Cut the tomatoes into thick slices and children can use a butter knife to cut them into smaller pieces. Panzanella makes a fine main dish in late summer, served on top of fresh salad greens.

Serves 4 to 6

4 to 6 cups day-old crusty bread, cubed or torn into 1-inch pieces

1½ pounds ripe tomatoes, cut into ½-inch pieces

1 slice red onion, diced

1 garlic clove, minced

½ cup fresh basil leaves, thinly sliced

¼ cup chopped fresh parsley

⅓ cup pitted Kalamata olives

3 tablespoons red wine vinegar

6 tablespoons olive oil

¼ teaspoon salt

½ teaspoon freshly ground black pepper

1 tablespoon capers (optional)

1 cucumber, peeled and cut into 1-inch pieces (optional)

½ roasted red bell pepper, thinly sliced (optional)

1 In a serving bowl, combine all the ingredients, except the vinegar, olive oil, and salt and pepper.

2 Drizzle the vinegar and olive oil and sprinkle the salt and pepper over the ingredients. Stir carefully and serve immediately.

What Kids Can Do

Tear bread into pieces

Slice tomatoes

Tear basil and parsley leaves

Cooks' Note

Make panzanella with lightly grilled or toasted bread.

Did You Know?

There is no doubt that the original panzanella salad came about as a way to use stale bread and an overabundance of ripe tomatoes in late summer. Traditionally it consisted of bread, tomatoes, onions, basil, wine vinegar, olive oil, salt, and pepper. The bread was torn or cut into pieces, soaked in water, and then squeezed out by hand.

Let's Grow Tomatoes!

Tomatoes grow in many shapes, sizes, and colors, from tiny Sweet 100 to Yellow Pear, orange Sungold, and yellow Russian Galina, to bright-red Early Girl, purple Black from Tula, or sweet, dark-pink Brandywine. There is even a huge striped tomato called Mortgage Lifter. The story goes that farmer Radiator Charlie, who developed this unusual tomato by crossing different varieties, was able to pay off the mortgage on his farm by selling many, many Mortgage Lifter tomato plants.

You can start tomatoes from seed indoors in late winter or early spring, but of course there are vigorous young plants to buy at farmers' markets, nurseries, and sometimes even grocery stores.

When the weather has warmed and there is no threat of frost it is time to transplant tomatoes into the garden. First, harden off the young plants by leaving them outside for a few hours a day. Gradually increase the time that they are outside, until after a week, they are outside all day and night. This process allows the plants to adjust to the sun and wind.

1 Dig a 6- to 8-inch-deep hole for each young tomato plant, and space them 3 feet apart.

2 Put several cups of compost into each hole and mix with the dirt.

3 Tap the plant out of its pot and put it into the ground.

4 Fill in around the plant with soil, pat gently but firmly, then make a slight well around the plant to help hold water.

5 Water the newly transplanted tomatoes thoroughly. Provide shade for the first several days, while the plants adapt to their new home.

6 Support the plants as they grow with cages or stakes. No directions are needed for harvesting, except to wait for the beautiful fruit to ripen.

Tomato Cucumber Salad

What Kids Can Do

Peel and slice cucumber

Wash and cut
bell pepper

Squeeze lemon juice

Measure and whisk
dressing

Crumble cheese

Cooks' Note

This salad can be eaten by itself, stuffed inside of pita breads, or served alongside Zucchini Cakes (page 12).

Did You Know?

The French were the first to use tomatoes in salads and called the beautiful red fruits *pommes d'amour* (apples of love).

This salad is dressed with a very simple mixture of olive oil and lemon juice. Since it has no lettuce, kids are often surprised that it's called a salad.

Serves 4

1 cucumber, peeled and sliced

2 Roma tomatoes, cut into ½-inch pieces

1 red or green bell pepper, cut into ¼-inch pieces

1 green onion, thinly sliced

½ cup Kalamata or California black olives (optional)

2 tablespoons chopped fresh parsley

3 tablespoons fresh lemon juice

3 tablespoons olive oil

½ cup crumbled feta cheese

1 Put all the ingredients in a serving bowl and stir lightly to combine. Serve immediately.

Sweet and Sour Cucumbers

This quick pickle goes really well with Chinese American Fried Rice (page 56). Rice vinegar is less harsh than white or cider vinegar and has just the right sweet tang.

Serves 4

> **1 large cucumber, peeled**
>
> **2 tablespoons rice vinegar**
>
> **1 tablespoon water**
>
> **1 teaspoon sugar**
>
> **¼ teaspoon salt**

(page 56)

> **What Kids Can Do**
>
> Peel and slice cucumber
>
> Measure and whisk dressing

1 Cut the cucumber in half lengthwise, then cut into ¼-inch-thick slices and put the slices into a serving bowl.

2 In a small bowl, whisk together the rice vinegar, water, sugar, and salt until the sugar and salt are completely dissolved. Pour the vinegar dressing over the cucumber slices and mix well. Serve as a side dish.

Let's Grow Cucumbers!

Cucumbers are in the same family of plants as watermelons. Like watermelons, cucumbers grow on vines and require warm weather, good soil, and consistent watering.

1 Plant cucumber seeds at least a week after the last spring frost.

2 Plant the seeds in rows, 1 inch deep and 6 to 10 inches apart. Cucumbers take 45 to 60 days from planting seeds until they are ready to pick.

3 To harvest, cut the cucumbers off the vine, rather than pulling or twisting them off the plant. If you have a bumper crop, share them with your friends and neighbors!

Did You Know?

Scientists believe that cucumbers first grew in the southern part of India over 4,000 years ago. There are about 100 varieties of cucumbers grown in the world today. They include many shapes, sizes, and colors—from the short and bumpy Kirby to the round and yellow Lemon cucumbers, to long and sweet Armenian cukes. Most cucumbers are eaten fresh, and others are made into pickles.

What kind of weather do cucumber plants need?

How many different varieties of cucumbers are grown in the world today?

How many kinds have you tasted?

What do you think happens to make a cucumber turn into a pickle?

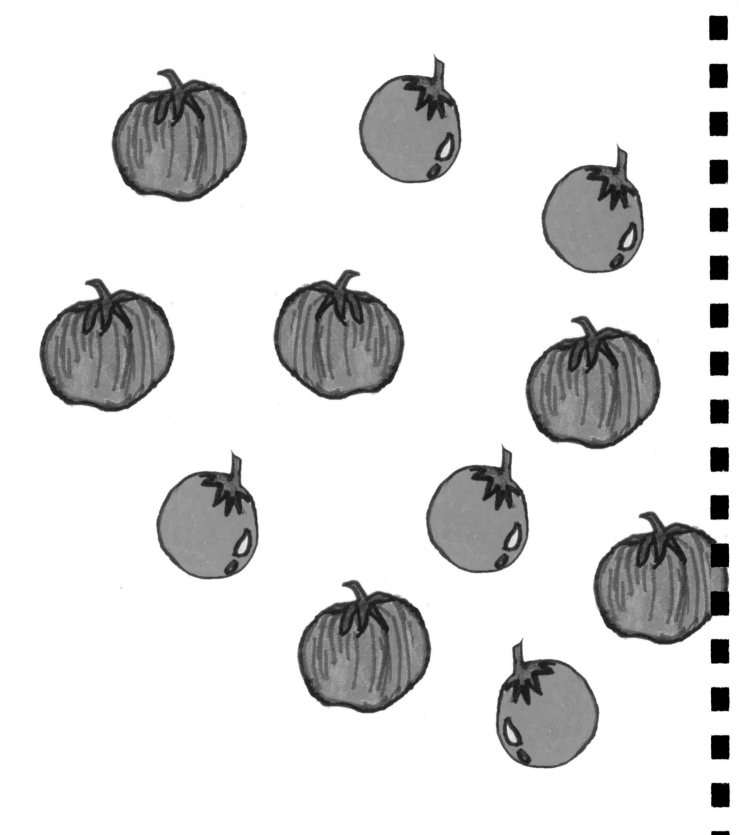

Main Dishes

Main Dishes

Recipes in this chapter reflect the rich and diverse cultural traditions that inspire us, with accompanying side dishes to make a full meal. From South American Llapingachos with Red Chile Sauce (page 44) to North African Tagine with Dressed-Up Couscous and Chermoula (page 80) to Fresh Green and White Fettuccine with Tomato Basil Sauce (page 90), these recipes are easy to prepare, and most use familiar ingredients but combine them in new or unexpected ways. Invite your children to wash vegetables, nibble a slice of fresh ginger, and measure pearly rice.

In our hurry-up lives, a main dish can be almost anything—a baked potato with freshly cooked broccoli and a squeeze of lemon, yesterday's pizza with salad greens from the garden, or a simple bowl of basmati rice topped with mildly spiced lentils. Look at what's in the fridge or pantry, or plan ahead with a list and a trip to a new grocery store or farmers' market. It can be fun to include your children in the planning.

Cooking together and gradually absorbing the process over time is one way to learn how to cook. Start by laying out all of the ingredients on the kitchen counter. Next, demonstrate how to cut the vegetables or fruits. Then stand together at the stove, and watch the magic of fire transform raw ingredients into a tasty dish to share. Applaud their efforts—and if one evening the kids really want to make scrambled eggs and toast, or popcorn and apples for dinner, remember to celebrate their growing independence!

South American Llapingachos with Red Chile Sauce

What Kids Can Do

Mash potatoes

Grate cheese

Tear parsley

Slice green onions

Make the patties

Cooks' Notes

✄ Serve with Red Chile Sauce (recipe follows) and Salad Greens with Creamy Lime Dressing (page 24) or Spinach Salad with Citrus Vinaigrette (page 28).

✄ Use Yukon Gold or other thin-skinned potatoes and there is no need to peel them. Just boil, mash, and go!

It's a lot like making mud pies. Everyone can lend a hand in mashing the potatoes, then forming the patties for this comforting dish. Originally from Ecuador, llapingachos (*ya-ping-ga-chose*) are traditionally served topped with fried eggs and a spicy peanut sauce.

Serves 4 to 6

2 pounds russet or other baking potatoes, boiled and cooled

4 ounces mozzarella or Monterey Jack cheese, grated

2 green onions, thinly sliced

2 tablespoons chopped fresh parsley

1½ cups corn kernels, fresh or frozen

¾ teaspoon salt

⅛ teaspoon freshly ground black pepper

Vegetable oil for griddle

1 Make the llapingachos: Peel the potatoes and put them into a large bowl. Use a potato masher to mash the potatoes. Add the grated cheese, green onions, parsley, corn, salt, and pepper. Stir until well combined. Form patties using ¼ cup of the potato mixture for each patty. Flatten the patties so that they are about ½ inch thick.

2 Cook the patties on a hot, well-oiled griddle for 3 to 4 minutes on each side, until dark golden brown and heated through. Remove from the heat and serve.

Red Chile Sauce

New Mexico red chile sauce is made from dried chile pods that are used whole or ground and then cooked with water or broth. In New Mexico, red chile sauce is traditionally made with pork, but we offer a vegetarian version here. A tip to bring out the spicy-sweet flavor: cook the sauce until the foam disappears.

Makes about 2 cups

3 garlic cloves, minced

2 tablespoons butter

2 tablespoons unbleached white flour

½ cup ground mild New Mexico red chile

2½ cups water

¾ teaspoon salt

¼ teaspoon freshly ground black pepper

⅛ teaspoon dried oregano

1 Put the garlic and butter into a saucepan over medium heat. Cook for about 30 seconds, stirring until the butter is melted and the garlic is fragrant but not brown.

2 Add the flour and cook for about 1 minute, whisking constantly. Whisk in the chile and cook only until fragrant. Be careful not to burn the chile or the sauce will taste bitter.

3 Slowly add the water, a little at a time, continuing to whisk constantly. Bring to a boil. Add the salt, pepper, and oregano.

4 Reduce the heat to low and simmer for 20 to 30 minutes, uncovered, until the foam disappears and the sauce thickens, stirring occasionally. Remove from the heat and serve.

> **What Kids Can Do**
>
> Peel garlic
>
> Measure ingredients
>
> Sprinkle salt and spices

Let's Grow Potatoes!

1   In late spring, dig 4-inch-deep trenches 2 to 3 feet apart.

2   Plant small "seed" potatoes 12 inches apart and cover with about 3 inches of soil.

3   When the shoots are about a foot tall, mound 6 to 8 inches of soil or straw mulch around the plants, since the potato tubers grow out from the stems.

4   Continue to water and watch.

5   When the potato plants flower, you can root around the edges to harvest a few tasty new potatoes. If you want larger spuds, wait until late summer or early fall when the plants' leaves begin to dry. Then comes the fun of digging for your buried treasure!

Did You Know?

Did you know that potatoes first grew in the Andes Mountains of Peru and were probably small, knobby shapes of a variety of colors, including purple, pink, blue, yellow, and red? Today there is a potato preserve in Peru, near the city of Cuzco, called "Parque de la Papa." The 22,000 acres, high in the Andes Mountains, are home to 6 villages and 8,000 people. More than 1,300 varieties of potatoes are grown there. Visitors can sign up for 1-, 3-, or 5-day tours where they meet with farmers, weavers, and cooks.

Black Bean Tostadas with Salsa Fresca

What Kids Can Do

Wash vegetables

Mash beans

Grate cheese
(watch those knuckles)

From sorting beans to measuring spices, from peeling and mincing garlic to sprinkling on toppings, there is lots for kids to do to help make this meal.

Serves 4 to 6

Black Beans

1 cup dry black beans, cooked, or 2 (15-ounce) cans

½ medium onion, chopped

2 garlic cloves, minced

2 tablespoons vegetable oil

½ teaspoon ground cumin

½ teaspoon salt

½ teaspoon fresh oregano or ¼ teaspoon dried oregano

1 Cook the black beans; or, if using canned beans, drain the juice from one can of black beans before putting all of the beans into a bowl. Use a potato masher to mash the beans until they are no longer whole. Set the mashed beans aside.

2 In a saucepan, heat the oil over medium-high heat. Add the onions and sauté for 1 to 2 minutes. Stir in the garlic and cumin and cook for 30 seconds more. Stir in the black beans.

3 When the beans begin to boil, reduce the heat to low, stir in the salt and oregano, and simmer for 10 minutes, uncovered. Keep warm until ready to serve.

Tostada Fixings

12 Corn Tortillas (page 104) or 12 store-bought corn tortillas or tostada shells

6 ounces mild cheddar cheese, grated

½ head Romaine lettuce, thinly sliced

Salsa Fresca (recipe follows)

1 Assemble and serve the tostadas: Warm the tortillas on a griddle or in the oven. Top each tortilla with a spoonful of black beans, and pass the cheese, lettuce, and salsa.

What Kids Can Do

Wash vegetables

Peel garlic

Squeeze lime juice

Slice tomatoes

Tear cilantro

Salsa Fresca

Salsa transcends culture, and it can now be found almost every-where. Homemade salsa is easy to make and is one of the tastiest ways to use the summer's bounty of tomatoes, chile, and fresh herbs.

Makes about 3 cups

Did You Know?

Salsa is the Spanish word for sauce.

5 medium tomatoes

3 garlic cloves, minced

⅓ cup minced red onion

3 tablespoons fresh lime juice

½ teaspoon salt

⅛ teaspoon freshly ground pepper

1 tablespoon chopped cilantro

1 to 2 jalapeños

1 Cut the tomatoes into ½-inch pieces and put into a bowl.

2 Add the garlic and onion to the tomatoes. Stir in the lime juice, salt, and pepper. Add the cilantro and stir only until combined.

3 Because hot peppers can burn the skin, an adult should seed and mince the jalapeños, then add them to the salsa.

Vegetable Tamales and Pinto Beans

What Kids Can Do

Wash vegetables

Tear cilantro

Grate zucchini and cheese
(watch those knuckles)

Mix masa

Wrap tamales

In Santa Fe, tamales are one of winter's best gifts. With everyone working together—mixing masa, tearing cilantro for the filling, and wrapping it all up in soft corn husks—a tamale party is a fun way to spend a snowy afternoon, and then you get to eat them! If tamales are new to you, remember to unwrap the little packages before eating.

Makes 24 small tamales

Wrappers and Masa

4 ounces dried corn husks

2¼ cups masa harina de maíz

¾ teaspoon salt

½ teaspoon baking powder

¼ cup unsalted butter, melted

1¾ cups warm water

Tamale Filling

2 mild green chiles (Anaheim), roasted, peeled, and diced

1 medium green or yellow summer squash, grated

1 cup frozen corn kernels

½ cup grated Monterey Jack cheese

2 tablespoons chopped cilantro

¼ teaspoon dried oregano

½ teaspoon salt

Cooks' Notes

☙ If Anaheim chiles are not available or roasting them seems too daunting, substitute a chopped bell pepper. The tamales might be a little less "authentic," but you won't lose any of the wonder of making them.

☙ Use fresh corn kernels in place of the frozen corn. Cut the corn off the cob. Add as is, or for a deeper flavor, pan-roast the corn before adding it to the filling: Heat a heavy skillet over medium-high heat. Add the corn and stir until it browns in spots and smells toasty.

☙ For heartier tamales, add 1½ cups shredded or chopped cooked chicken or turkey to the filling.

☙ Serve with Red Chile Sauce (page 45) and Pinto Beans (recipe follows).

50

1   Soak the corn husks in hot water until soft and pliable. Tear 3 corn husks into ¼-inch strips to be used to tie the tamales.

2   Make the masa (dough): Put the masa harina de maíz, baking powder, and salt into a bowl and mix together. Stir in the melted butter. Add the warm water and mix well to make a soft dough. In the bowl, knead the dough gently for 1 minute. Cover the masa and let rest for 10 minutes.

3   Make the tamale filling: In a bowl, mix together the green chile, summer squash, corn, cheese, cilantro, oregano, and salt. Stir well to combine.

4   Assemble the tamales: Remove the corn husks from the water and pat them dry. Lay a softened corn husk flat on a clean surface. Put a heaping tablespoon of masa in the center of the corn husk. Flatten masa with fingertips to about ⅛ inch thick. Put a heaping teaspoon of filling into the center of the masa. Roll up and tie the ends of the tamale with the corn husk strips.

5   Fill a large pot with about 3 inches of water. Insert a vegetable steamer basket, pasta insert, or colander that fits inside the pot. Bring water to a boil over high heat.

6   Place the tamales in the steamer so that they are standing up. Cook for 25 minutes. Check to make sure there is still enough water in the pan as the tamales steam.

Did You Know?

There are many, many kinds of tamales! Some are wrapped in fresh corn leaves, banana leaves, or avocado leaves. While most tamales have fillings of meat, cheese, or beans, some have no filling at all.

Tamale

How to Roast and Peel Chiles

Note: This is not an activity for small children. Be careful not to rub your eyes while working with chiles. If your skin is sensitive, wear gloves for peeling the chiles.

1 Place chiles directly on the grate over a gas burner on the stove top. Turn the burner on to medium-high heat. Use tongs to rotate the chiles as the skin begins to puff and brown. When the chiles are almost completely brown and blistered, remove from the heat, wrap in paper towels, and place in a plastic bag.

2 Let the chiles steam and cool in the bag until they can be easily handled. Remove from the bag and unwrap.

3 Slit the chile lengthwise to remove the seeds. Carefully rub the chiles to remove the darkened skins. Don't worry if some of the skin doesn't come off—that just adds to the flavor!

What did you do next? What did you see, smell, and taste?

Pinto Beans

Beans are basic, inexpensive, and nutritious, and they can be seasoned in so many ways. Some people like very plain beans, with just a bit of salt, or you can spice them up with ground cumin, garlic, sautéed onion, and red chile.

Serves about 6

2 cups dry pinto beans

8 cups water

½ teaspoon oregano

1 teaspoon salt, or to taste

¼ teaspoon freshly ground black pepper

2 tablespoons olive oil

2 to 3 cloves garlic, chopped

1 Sort the beans to remove any little stones. Rinse, then cover with water to soak for several hours or overnight. Drain and rinse.

2 In a large pot, bring the water to a boil over high heat. Add the beans and cook, skimming off any foam that appears.

3 Reduce the heat to low, partially cover, and cook until tender, about 2 hours. Add the oregano, salt, and pepper.

4 Sauté the garlic in the olive oil, until just fragrant. Stir the garlic into the beans, then simmer over low heat for 10 to 20 minutes more to combine the flavors.

What Kids Can Do

Sort and rinse beans

Measure ingredients

Add herbs and salt

Cooking Beans

Children love the feel of dry beans—cool and smooth—and can help to clean the beans by sorting out any tiny rocks. One cup of dry beans will make about 3 cups cooked beans (about the same amount as in two 15-ounce cans).

Most cooks agree that freshly shelled dry beans (from the current season) will cook more quickly than last year's beans. Early fall is a good time to find freshly dried beans at your local farmers' market. You may not have acres of beans in your backyard, but it is fun for children to shell even a few. Or alternatively, if you grow any type of green beans, allow some to mature and dry on the plant. Then, when fall comes, harvest the dry pods and shell them with your children at the kitchen table or in front of a crackling fire. Adding even a few of these homegrown beans will add a special touch to any soup.

Chinese American Fried Rice

What Kids Can Do

Grate carrots

Shell peas

Measure rice

Peel garlic

Tear cabbage

Cut the egg pancake
and arrange the pieces
on top of the fried rice

Six-year-olds have been known to devour this colorful dish! Invite them to help assemble all of the ingredients, break and whisk the eggs, and if you're lucky enough to have fresh peas from your garden or farmers' market, shell the peas.

Serves 4 to 6

Rice

2 cups water

1 cup jasmine or long grain white rice

½ teaspoon salt

Egg Pancake

2 eggs

½ teaspoon water

2 teaspoons vegetable oil

Vegetables and Other Ingredients for Fried Rice

1 tablespoon vegetable oil

1 garlic clove, minced

1 teaspoon peeled and minced fresh ginger

1 carrot, coarsely grated or cut into matchsticks

1 zucchini, diced into ¼-inch pieces

1½ cups cabbage, cut or torn into ¾-inch pieces

2 tablespoons soy sauce

1 cup fresh (see note opposite) or frozen peas

1 green onion, thinly sliced

1 Cook the rice: In a saucepan, bring the water to a boil over high heat. Add the rice and salt, return to a boil, and cover. Reduce the heat to low and cook rice, covered, until all the liquid has been absorbed, about 20 minutes. Let the rice sit for at least 5 minutes.

2 Make the egg pancake: In a bowl, whisk together the eggs and water. Heat a large skillet over high heat and add 2 teaspoons of vegetable oil. Pour the eggs into the pan. Cook over medium-high heat for about 2 minutes. Cover the pan and continue to cook for 1 minute more, until the egg pancake is set. Turn the pancake out onto a cutting board and cut into strips.

3 Finish the fried rice: Heat 1 tablespoon of vegetable oil in a large skillet over medium-high heat. Add the garlic, ginger, and carrots and cook for about 1 minute. Add the zucchini, cabbage, and soy sauce. Cover and cook for about 3 minutes more. Stir in the peas and green onions, reduce the heat to medium, and stir in the rice. Remove from the heat. Place the strips of egg pancake on top. Serve immediately.

Cooks' Notes

⚘ Serve with Sweet and Sour Cucumbers (page 37).

⚘ If using fresh peas: Remove the peas from the pods. Cook the peas in boiling water until they turn bright green. Drain, rinse in cold water, and add to the fried rice as directed.

⚘ Substitute 1 to 2 cups of sugar snap peas for the green peas.

⚘ Add ½ pound cooked shrimp when you are finishing the fried rice.

Let's Grow Peas!

All peas, but especially English peas, are made for tiny hands. English peas require shelling to find the delicious green gems that grow inside. Snow peas are flat, with crisp edible pods, and are often used in oriental dishes; snap peas have sweet and plump edible pods.

1. Plant peas in early spring, as they need cool weather to grow. Pea plants grow into either short bush plants (2 to 3 feet tall) or tall climbing vines (4 to 6 feet tall). Before planting, decide which best suits your garden site. Peas like reasonably good garden soil that has been enriched with organic matter, but they are not terribly fussy.

2. Soak the pea seeds overnight before planting, which will improve germination. Children love to see how the seeds "grow," getting bigger as they absorb the water. Hoe a wide furrow, then make a zigzag pattern of the seeds, planting each seed 1 to 1½ inches apart in the furrow. Cover the seeds with about 1 inch of soil. Don't worry if some of the seeds are too close together. One of the wonderful things about peas is that they don't need thinning!

3. Water thoroughly for the first few days, then as needed to keep the soil moist but not soggy. After the peas sprout, continue watering so that the soil stays somewhat moist, about every 3 to 5 days. For tall pea varieties, plant alongside an existing fence that they can climb, or provide a trellis or pole tepee. It is easiest to put up climbing structures before planting or while the plants are small. If you have planted bush peas, supports are not necessary.

4. The most effective way to pick peas is to use two hands, one to hold the plant and one to pick the pea. This keeps the plant from being pulled out of the ground, a difficult concept for young children. Climbing peas are easier to pick than bush peas because the plants are clinging to a structure.

Note: Be aware that children younger than three years old can choke on raw peas.

Japanese Rice Bowl

What Kids Can Do

Wash rice

Wash vegetables

Peel carrots

Peel and mince garlic and ginger

Tear nori

Cooks' Note

Substitute short grain brown rice for the white rice in this recipe. Unless it is quick-cooking brown rice, it will take longer to cook.

Traditionally, a bowl of white rice is part of every meal in Japan, even breakfast! Vary the vegetables as you like, perhaps including baby greens from your garden. Kids can peel carrots, measure ingredients, and crumble the papery nori into tiny pieces for garnish.

Rice

1½ cups short grain white rice

3 cups water

½ teaspoon salt

Vegetables

2 tablespoons vegetable oil

1 teaspoon peeled and minced fresh ginger

2 garlic cloves, minced

3 carrots, peeled and thinly sliced

½ cup shelled edamame

1 red bell pepper, cut into thin strips about ½ inch long

3 to 4 heads baby bok choy, cut into 1-inch pieces

3 tablespoons soy sauce

2 tablespoons rice vinegar

1 green onion, thinly sliced

1 sheet toasted nori, crumbled into small pieces (optional)

2 tablespoons sesame seeds, toasted

1   Make the rice: Put the rice into a bowl with cool water. Swirl the rice around and then pour off the water. Repeat this process twice, until the water is clear.

2   In a medium saucepan, bring the water and salt to a boil over high heat. Add the rice and return to boiling. Reduce heat to low, cover, and cook for 15 to 18 minutes, until all the water is absorbed and the rice is completely cooked. Do not stir.

3   Remove from the heat and allow the rice to sit, covered, for about 10 minutes.

4   Cook the vegetables: Heat the vegetable oil in a skillet over medium-high heat. Add the ginger, garlic, carrots, and edamame and cook for 2 to 3 minutes, stirring often. Add the bell peppers and bok choy.

5   Cover and cook for several minutes more, until the vegetables are cooked but still crisp. Remove from the heat and stir in the soy sauce and green onions.

6   Toast the sesame seeds in a small skillet over medium-high heat, stirring constantly until lightly browned. Remove from the heat.

7   Serve the rice topped with a spoonful of vegetables and a sprinkling of toasted sesame seeds and nori.

How many words can you make using the letters in the word "chopsticks"?

Vegetable Paella

What Kids Can Do

Wash vegetables

Measure ingredients

Tear parsley leaves

Cut tomatoes and bell pepper

Cooks' Note

Serve with Salad Greens (page 24) with Lemony Dressing (page 22).

Did You Know?

In Spain, after all of the ingredients are added to the paella pan, the rice is never stirred—so it forms a delicious brown crust on the bottom of the pan. This crust is called *la socarrat* and is considered a special treat.

Our version of this famous rice dish from Spain is a twist on the original, which is traditionally cooked in a shallow pan over an open fire and nearly always features meat and seafood. This paella is much lighter than most, with just a hint of fragrant saffron.

Serves 4 to 6

1 tablespoon olive oil

½ medium white onion, chopped

1 red or green bell pepper, diced

1 cup medium grain white rice

¼ teaspoon turmeric

2 cups broth, chicken or vegetable

2 medium tomatoes, diced, or ½ cup canned diced tomatoes

¼ teaspoon salt

⅛ teaspoon paprika

⅛ teaspoon dried thyme

5 saffron threads

1 cup frozen peas

2 tablespoons chopped fresh parsley

1 In a large skillet or paella pan, heat the olive oil over medium-high heat. Add the onion and bell pepper and cook for 2 to 3 minutes, stirring often until the vegetables have softened. Stir in the rice and turmeric and cook for 1 minute more.

2 Add the broth, tomatoes, salt, paprika, thyme, and saffron. Bring to a boil, stir once, cover, and reduce the heat to low. Cook for 25 to 30 minutes, until all the liquid has been absorbed.

3 Add the peas and parsley, but do not stir. Remove from the heat and let sit, covered, for 5 to 10 minutes before serving. Stir to combine and serve immediately.

Did You Know?

Saffron is the most expensive spice in the world. Saffron threads are the dried stigmas on the inside of a saffron crocus flower. Only a very tiny amount of saffron is needed to flavor a dish. The saffron crocus flower blooms in fall and must be picked by hand in the early morning.

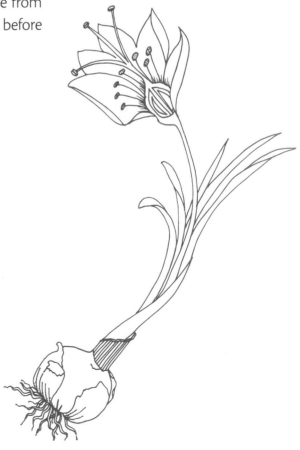

Middle Eastern Falafel with Yogurt Mint Sauce

What Kids Can Do

Wash parsley

Mash garbanzo beans

Measure herbs and spices

Juice lemon

Cooks' Notes

- Serve with Yogurt Mint Sauce (recipe follows) and Mediterranean Flatbread (page 110).

- A food processor works fast to grind the garbanzo beans, but children do love to use their energy by mashing the beans in a bowl using an old-fashioned potato masher.

- Consider investing in a small, simple citrus juicer. It makes squeezing fresh juice a breeze and might even inspire you to make lemonade.

Falafel is made from a mixture of ground garbanzo beans, spices, lemon juice, and plenty of parsley, shaped into balls and deep fried. A popular form of street food in many Middle Eastern countries, falafel is usually served wrapped in soft, thick pita bread drizzled with tahini sauce. Our falafel are cooked on a griddle and use just a little oil. Kids have fun mashing the garbanzo beans and making the falafel into patties. The argument will be over who gets to squeeze the lemons!

Serves 4 to 6

1 cup garbanzo beans, cooked, or 2 (15-ounce) cans, drained and rinsed

3 tablespoons lemon juice

⅔ cup finely chopped fresh parsley

2 green onions, thinly sliced

¾ teaspoon salt

¼ teaspoon ground cumin

½ teaspoon turmeric

⅛ teaspoon cayenne pepper

¼ teaspoon dried thyme

1 egg, beaten

1 tablespoon olive oil

2 tablespoons unbleached white flour

Olive oil for cooking

1 Put the garbanzo beans into a bowl and use a potato masher to completely mash them. Stir the lemon juice, parsley, and green onions into the mashed garbanzo beans. Add the salt, cumin, turmeric, cayenne, thyme, egg, and olive oil and mix well. Stir in the flour.

2 Form the falafel mixture into patties about ½ inch thick and 2 inches in diameter.

3 Heat 2 tablespoons of oil on a griddle over medium-high heat. Cook the patties for about 3 minutes on each side, until dark golden brown and cooked through.

Yogurt Mint Sauce

Tearing up fresh mint leaves releases a fragrance that sweetly envelops the cooks. Make this green-flecked sauce with your favorite plain or Greek yogurt.

Makes about 1 cup

> **1 cup plain yogurt**
> **2 tablespoons minced fresh mint leaves**
> **⅛ teaspoon salt**
> **⅛ teaspoon freshly ground black pepper**

1 In a bowl, stir together the yogurt, mint, salt, and pepper.

What Kids Can Do

Wash and tear
mint leaves

Measure ingredients

Stir sauce

Cooks' Notes

In addition to serving this sauce with falafel, it makes a great salad dressing or vegetable dip.

Falafel Poem

Make a poem using the letters of the word "falafel." Make each letter of "falafel" the first letter of the first word in the line. One idea might be to write a poem about cooking, or you could write a poem about the kinds of foods you like to eat.

F

A

L

A

F

E

L

Red Lentils with Carrot Rice Pilaf and Cucumber Raita

What Kids Can Do

Measure ingredients

Peel garlic

Tear or chop
cilantro leaves

Cooks' Note

Serve with Carrot Rice Pilaf
and Cucumber Raita
(recipes follow) and
Chapatis (page 119).

Did You Know?

In India, lentils and rice are
everyday foods for millions
of people, and people have
been eating lentils for thousands of years. There are
many kinds of lentils, from
tiny red lentils, black lentils,
and speckled French lentils,
to larger golden-yellow,
green, and brown lentils.

Thousands of kids eat lentils in Santa Fe! Children enjoy grinding the
toasted cumin seeds with a mortar and pestle and tearing up the
cilantro leaves.

Serves 4

1 cup red lentils

4 cups water

4 medium tomatoes, diced

½ teaspoon salt

2 tablespoons butter

2 garlic cloves, minced

¾ teaspoon cumin seeds

2 teaspoons ground mild red chile or ¼ teaspoon freshly
ground black pepper

½ teaspoon ground coriander

2 tablespoons chopped cilantro

1 Combine the lentils and water in a saucepan. Bring to a
boil over high heat. Skim off the foam that appears.
Reduce the heat to low, partially cover, and simmer 30 to
45 minutes, stirring occasionally, until tender. Add water
as needed to keep the lentils covered as they cook.

2 Add the tomatoes and salt and simmer 5 to 10 minutes.

3 In a skillet, melt the butter over medium-high heat. Add the garlic and cumin seeds and sauté until fragrant but not brown. Add the chile and coriander and stir for 20 seconds more. Stir the spice mixture into the lentils.

4 Just before serving, stir in the cilantro.

Cucumber Raita

Kids can measure, grate, and mix to make this cool and refreshing sauce.

Makes about 2 cups

>**1 small cucumber**
>
>**1½ cups plain yogurt**
>
>**½ teaspoon ground cumin**
>
>**½ teaspoon minced cilantro**
>
>**2 teaspoons minced fresh mint (optional)**
>
>**¼ teaspoon salt**

1 Peel the cucumber. Using the side of a grater with the largest holes, grate the cucumber.

2 Whisk the yogurt in a bowl until smooth, then stir in the rest of the ingredients.

What Kids Can Do

Peel and grate cucumber
(watch those knuckles)

Tear cilantro
and mint leaves

Whisk ingredients
together

Let's Grow Coriander!

The coriander plant has two different parts that are used in cooking: the delicate green leaves, which we call cilantro, and the seeds.

1   Plant coriander seeds in late spring in good garden soil.

2   Sow the seeds about ¼ inch deep, 6 to 8 inches apart. Cover the seeds with soil and water well.

3   Water every day until the seeds sprout, which will take about 2 weeks.

4   Begin to harvest individual stems and leaves when the plants are 6 inches tall. When the plants begin to flower, the lacy white blossoms can be used as a garnish for soups or salads.

5   After flowering, the seeds will form and can be used in cooking or saved to plant the next year!

Carrot Rice Pilaf

Pilaf is a dish made of rice, or another grain, that is cooked with other ingredients, or in a seasoned broth. Kids love to grate the carrots and toss in the cinnamon stick, which produces a familiar aroma while the rice cooks. They marvel at how the color from the carrots turns the rice a golden yellow.

Serves 4 as a side dish

1 cup basmati rice

1 tablespoon butter

½ cup peeled and grated carrot

2¼ cups water

1 cinnamon stick

½ teaspoon salt

1 Put the rice into a bowl with cool water. Swirl the rice around and then pour off the water. Repeat this process 2 or 3 times, until the water is clear.

2 In a saucepan, melt the butter over medium-high heat. Add the rice and grated carrots and sauté for 2 minutes. Add the water, cinnamon stick, and salt. Bring to a boil.

3 Reduce the heat to medium and simmer, uncovered, for 2 minutes. Reduce the heat to low and cover. Cook the rice for about 20 minutes, until all of the liquid has been absorbed. Remove from the heat. Let the rice rest for 10 minutes before serving.

What Kids Can Do

Measure ingredients

Wash rice

Grate carrots
(watch those knuckles)

Ethiopian Lentils with Tikil Gomen

What Kids Can Do

Grind spices

Peel garlic

Measure ingredients

Tear collard greens

Cooks' Notes

✧ Serve with Tikil Gomen (recipe follows) and Injera (page 118).

✧ Berbere can also be purchased already made at specialty stores or spice shops.

Children really enjoy the action of grinding whole spices for the berbere spice mix with a mortar and pestle. It's fun to notice the colors, shapes, and sizes of the seeds, and to discover the exotic aromas as the seeds are ground into powder.

Serves 4 to 6

Berbere

1 whole clove

1 cardamom pod

3 black peppercorns

2 whole allspices

¼ teaspoon whole cumin seeds

⅛ teaspoon whole fenugreek seeds

1 teaspoon ground mild red chile

⅛ teaspoon ground ginger

⅛ teaspoon ground nutmeg

⅛ teaspoon ground turmeric

¼ teaspoon salt

Lentils

1 tablespoon butter

½ cup chopped red onion

2 garlic cloves, minced

1 cup green or brown lentils, cooked, or 2 (15-ounce) cans

3 large collard leaves

1 Make the berbere: Remove the seeds from the cardamom pod. Combine the clove, cardamom seeds, peppercorns, allspices, and fenugreek seeds in a small skillet and toast over medium-high heat, stirring constantly until the spices become fragrant. Remove from the heat and let the spices cool.

2 Grind the spices with a mortar and pestle until finely ground. Transfer the spices into a small bowl and stir in the ground ginger, nutmeg, turmeric, and salt.

3 Make the lentils: In a saucepan, melt the butter over medium-high heat. Add the onions and garlic and cook for about 2 minutes, until the onions have softened. Add the berbere and cook, stirring constantly for about 30 seconds more. Add the cooked lentils along with the juice. When the lentils begin to boil, reduce the heat to medium and simmer for 5 minutes, uncovered.

4 Chop or tear the collard greens into 1-inch pieces. Stir the collards into the lentils and cook, covered, for about 10 minutes more, until the collards are tender.

Did You Know?

Spices come from dried roots, leaves, or barks of trees or the buds, stems, and seeds of plants. Black pepper, cinnamon, cardamom, and cumin originally grew in Asia, and chiles first grew in the Americas. Long ago, spices were traded as people traveled throughout the world on ships. The spice trade began in the Middle East about 4,000 years ago. It's hard to imagine today just how valuable spices were in past centuries, and how the search for spices shaped the history of the world.

Tikil Gomen

What Kids Can Do

Wash and cut vegetables

Tear cabbage

Peel and mince garlic

Tikil gomen combines greens such as kale, collard greens, or cabbage with other vegetables. Carrots are a colorful addition to this lightly spiced Ethiopian vegetable dish. There's magic in stirring in the turmeric and watching what happens.

Serves 4 to 6 as a side dish

1 tablespoon peeled and minced fresh ginger

3 garlic cloves

½ medium onion, cut into ¼-inch pieces

1 carrot, cut into ¼-inch pieces

2 Yukon Gold potatoes, cut into ½-inch pieces

3 tablespoons olive oil

½ teaspoon turmeric

½ teaspoon cumin seeds, toasted

1½ cups water

1 jalapeño

½ head cabbage

½ teaspoon salt

1 Heat the olive oil in a pot over medium heat. Add the ginger, garlic, onion, carrot, and potatoes and cook for 5 to 7 minutes, stirring often. Stir in the cumin seeds and turmeric and cook for 1 to 2 minutes more. Add the water and stir to combine. Reduce the heat and cook, covered, for about 10 minutes.

2 Because they can burn the skin, an adult should cut the jalapeño in half and remove the seeds. Add the jalapeño to the pot.

3 Tear the cabbage leaves into ¾-inch pieces to equal about 6 cups. Stir in the cabbage and salt and cook, covered, for about 5 minutes more, until the cabbage is tender and the potatoes are cooked through. Remove from the heat.

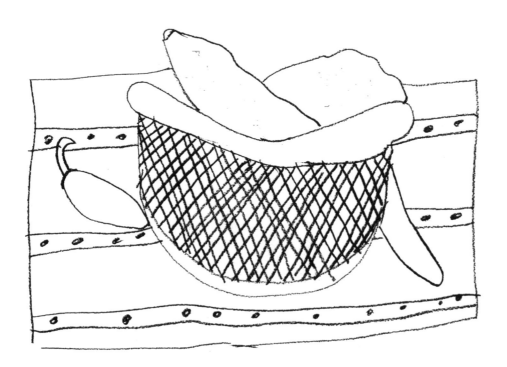

Draw a picture of your family eating together.

North African Tagine with Dressed-Up Couscous and Chermoula

What Kids Can Do

Wash vegetables

Grind pepper

Measure spices

"Tagine" is the name of an earthenware pot with a wide, shallow bottom and a dome-shaped top, and it is also the name of the stews that are cooked in it, usually over a fire. This version is made with sweetly spiced carrots, sweet potatoes, parsnips, and turnips. Little kids enjoy washing the vegetables: Fill a tub with several inches of lukewarm water. Put the vegetables into the tub, and demonstrate how to use a vegetable brush. You may have to ask them to stop scrubbing!

Serves 6

Cooks' Notes

✁ Serve with Dressed-Up Couscous and Chermoula (recipes follow).

✁ An easy way to peel fresh ginger is to scrape the dull edge of a butter knife or a chopstick over the ginger root.

2 tablespoons butter

2 teaspoons minced fresh ginger root

1 onion, chopped into ¼-inch pieces

1 teaspoon ground turmeric

2 sweet potatoes, cut into ¾-inch pieces (about 5 cups)

2 carrots, peeled and cut into ¼-inch-thick slices

1 parsnip, peeled and cut into ¼-inch-thick slices

1 turnip, peeled and cut into ½-inch pieces

½ teaspoon ground cumin

¼ teaspoon ground coriander

1 teaspoon ground mild red chile

1 teaspoon salt

¼ teaspoon freshly ground black pepper

4 cups broth, chicken or vegetable

1 cinnamon stick

½ cup dry garbanzo beans, cooked, or 1 (15-ounce) can, drained and rinsed

1   Melt the butter in a large pot over medium-high heat. Add the ginger, onion, and turmeric, and sauté for about 4 minutes, stirring often, until the onions are soft and golden. Add the sweet potatoes, carrots, turnip, parsnip, cumin, coriander, red chile, salt, and pepper. Continue to cook, stirring constantly, for about 2 minutes, just until the spices are fragrant.

2   Add the broth and cinnamon stick, stirring to combine. Bring to a boil, and then reduce the heat to medium-low and cover. Simmer for about 20 minutes, stirring occasionally, until the vegetables are cooked through and tender. Add the garbanzo beans and cook for 5 minutes more. Remove the cinnamon stick before serving.

Did You Know?

History and spices go hand in hand. Morocco was a stopping place on spice-trade routes established thousands of years ago between Europe and the Far East. Spices like cinnamon, cumin, and paprika have long been an essential part of Moroccan cooking.

Write a letter to a faraway friend or family member.

Dear

Today, we cooked food from North

The dish was called

We cut carrots, turnips, parsnips, and

We added different

It was fun to

Sincerely,

Dressed-Up Couscous

This version of the tiniest pasta adds raisins and almonds for texture and variety. Use either whole wheat or white couscous—both are surprisingly light.

Serves 6

1½ cups water

1½ cups couscous

¼ teaspoon salt

3 tablespoons golden raisins

¼ cup slivered almonds, toasted

2 tablespoons chopped fresh cilantro

1 In a saucepan, bring the water to a boil over high heat. Add the couscous, salt, and golden raisins. Stir once. Cover the pan and turn off the heat.

2 Let the couscous sit for 10 to 15 minutes. Fluff the couscous with a fork. Gently stir in the almonds and cilantro.

What Kids Can Do

Measure ingredients

Tear cilantro leaves

Did You Know?

Couscous is a main food in North Africa. It is made from durum wheat, the same type of high-protein wheat that is used to make many other pastas. First, the wheat is ground into flour. Then the flour is mixed with a little water, rolled into tiny balls, and steamed. Long ago, women made couscous by hand, rolling the moistened flour with the palms of their hands in a flat basket. These days most couscous is made by machines.

What Kids Can Do

Wash and tear
cilantro leaves

Peel garlic

Grind the ingredients
for the sauce using a
mortar and pestle

Did You Know?

Moroccan mint tea—
green tea brewed with
fresh mint—is a popular
and traditional drink in
Morocco. Tea is often
served in small glasses and
sweetened with lumps of
sugar!

Chermoula

Emerald-green chermoula from Morocco makes a tasty topping for
vegetables or a tangy marinade for white fish or chicken. Using a
mortar and pestle is a hands-on way for kids to make the sauce, but
of course a food processor or blender works fine too.

Makes about 1 cup

> **2 cups chopped cilantro leaves**
>
> **1 garlic clove, minced**
>
> **½ teaspoon salt**
>
> **⅛ teaspoon freshly ground black pepper**
>
> **½ teaspoon ground cumin**
>
> **¼ teaspoon ground red chile or paprika**
>
> **¼ cup olive oil**

1 In a mortar and pestle, grind the garlic, salt, pepper,
cumin, and red chile to form a paste.

2 Add the cilantro leaves in small amounts and grind until
the mixture forms a paste.

3 Stir in the olive oil and lemon juice until well combined.
Chermoula will stay fresh for several days if it is stored,
tightly covered, in the refrigerator.

Potatoes Persillade

What Kids Can Do

Wash potatoes and cabbage

Chop parsley

Mince garlic

Grate lemon zest

Cooks' Notes

- Make homemade bread crumbs from leftover slices of bread.

- Serve with Spinach Salad with Citrus Vinaigrette (page 28).

- Use cauliflower, cut into small florets, instead of cabbage.

Tiny fingers are perfect for stripping thyme or parsley leaves from their stems and tearing bread into crumbs for the topping for this comforting dish. The French word *persillade* refers to a topping made with parsley (*persil* in French) and garlic that is commonly used to add a bright flavor to simple foods.

Serves 4 to 6

Potatoes and Cabbage

2 pounds red potatoes, cut into ¼-inch-thick slices

3 cups green cabbage, cut or torn into 1-inch pieces

2 tablespoons butter

¾ teaspoon salt

⅛ teaspoon freshly ground black pepper

1 teaspoon minced fresh thyme

Persillade (Parsley Topping)

2 tablespoons olive oil

1 or more garlic cloves, minced

1½ cups whole wheat bread crumbs

½ cup chopped fresh parsley

1 teaspoon lemon zest

1 Cook the potatoes in a large pot of boiling water over high heat for 15 to 20 minutes, until the potatoes are almost tender.

2 Add the cabbage and cook for about 5 minutes more, until bright green. Drain the potatoes and cabbage in a colander and then return them to the pot. Add the butter, salt, pepper, and thyme.

3 Make the persillade: In a skillet, heat the olive oil over medium-high heat. Add the garlic and bread crumbs. Cook over medium heat, stirring often, until the bread crumbs are toasted, about 5 to 8 minutes. Stir in the parsley and lemon zest and remove from the heat.

4 Serve the potatoes and cabbage topped with the persillade.

Let's Grow Cabbage!

Annual "giant cabbage" contests are still held in many places—with prizewinners ranging from 29 to 138 pounds! Cabbage is one vegetable that will stay tender and sweet no matter what the size, as long as the plants have cool weather and are given consistent water.

1 For a fall harvest, plant cabbage about 3 months before the first fall frost.

2 Plant the seeds ½ inch deep in rows about 3 feet apart.

3 Unless you're growing one of the giant varieties, thin the small cabbage plants when about 4 inches tall to have about 18 inches between plants.

4 Cabbages will be ready to harvest in the fall, when the heads become firm. They will have beautiful outer leaves that you don't see when you buy them in the store.

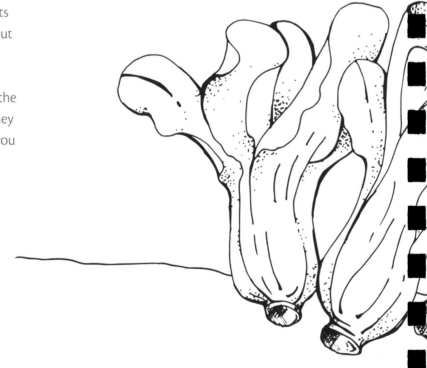

Fresh Green and White Fettuccine with Tomato Basil Sauce

What Kids Can Do

Measure, mix, knead, and roll out dough

Operate the hand-crank pasta machine

Making pasta is so exciting that children will want to do it all—from mixing the dough to rolling and cutting the noodles. They tell us that the green fettuccine tastes the best! Kids delight in working an old-fashioned hand-crank pasta machine, but it is surprisingly easy to roll out the dough with a rolling pin and to cut the noodles by hand.

Serves 6

Cooks' Notes

- Serve with Tomato Basil Sauce (recipe follows) and Tricolor Salad with Balsamic Vinaigrette (page 22).

- Semolina flour can be purchased in natural-food stores or specialty grocery stores.

White Fettuccine

1 cup unbleached white flour

1 cup semolina flour

¼ teaspoon salt

1 egg, lightly beaten

½ teaspoon olive oil

⅓ cup + 1 tablespoon water

Green Fettuccine

1 cup fresh spinach leaves, washed

1 cup unbleached white flour

1 cup semolina flour

¼ teaspoon salt

1 egg, lightly beaten

½ teaspoon olive oil

⅓ cup water

1   Make white fettuccine dough: In a bowl, mix together the white flour, semolina flour, and salt. In a separate bowl, whisk together the egg, oil, and water. Add the wet ingredients to the dry mixture and stir together until a rough-looking dough forms. On a clean, lightly floured work surface knead the dough for 2 to 3 minutes, until it is no longer sticky. Cover the dough with a clean cloth and let it rest for 5 minutes. Cut the dough into 8 equal pieces.

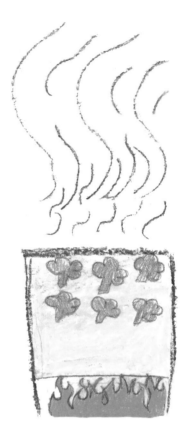

2   Make green fettuccine dough: In a small saucepan, heat a small amount of water until boiling. Add the spinach and cook, covered, for 1 to 2 minutes, until the spinach is wilted but still bright green. Use a strainer to drain the spinach, squeezing out as much liquid as possible. Chop the spinach. Follow the instructions for the white fettuccine dough, but add the chopped spinach to the egg, olive oil, and water. Follow the directions for mixing, kneading, and cutting the white fettuccine dough.

Using a Hand-Crank Pasta Machine

1   Follow the instructions that came with the pasta machine to roll the dough into sheets and then to cut the dough to make fettuccine.

2   Hang the fettuccine over a clean broomstick or lay it in a single layer on cookie sheets dusted with semolina flour so that the pasta doesn't stick together.

Making the Fettuccine by Hand

1 On a clean work surface dusted with semolina flour, roll the dough into a flat rectangular shape. Fold the dough into thirds and roll again. Repeat this folding and rolling process until the dough is very smooth and is about 1/16 inch thick (four or five times).

2 Sprinkle the finished piece of dough with semolina flour and loosely roll it up—like a burrito. Use a sharp knife to slice through the rolled pasta dough every ¼ inch.

3 Carefully unroll the fettuccine and hang as described above. Roll, fold, and cut the remaining pieces of dough.

Cook the Fettuccine

1 In a large pot, bring 12 cups of water to a boil over high heat.

2 Add ½ teaspoon of salt. Add the fettuccine and stir once or twice.

3 Cook over high heat, uncovered, for 3 to 5 minutes, until "al dente." Drain the pasta in a colander and serve immediately, topped with Tomato Basil Sauce and freshly grated cheese.

Tomato Basil Sauce

Garlic, olive oil, ripe tomatoes, and fresh basil are all it takes to make this summertime sauce. Even toddlers will enjoy tearing green basil leaves and smashing garlic cloves to loosen the papery skins.

Makes about 3 cups

1 tablespoon olive oil

3 garlic cloves, minced

10 to 12 medium tomatoes, diced

¼ teaspoon salt

⅛ teaspoon freshly ground black pepper

3 tablespoons chopped fresh basil leaves

Small wedge of Asiago or Parmesan cheese

1 In a saucepan, heat the olive oil and garlic over medium-high heat. Sauté for 10 seconds, until fragrant but not browned. Add the diced tomatoes and stir to combine.

2 Reduce the heat to medium, cover, and let simmer for about 10 minutes, until the mixture becomes juicy. Remove from the heat and stir in the salt, pepper, and basil.

3 Grate the cheese, using the medium- or small-holed side of a grater.

Let's Grow Herbs!

Herb plants are just the right size for toddlers and small children to explore because they are closer to the ground than adults! Young children will touch and grab as they explore, but they can learn rather quickly to be gentle with plants. Try growing a few fragrant perennial herbs, which grow year after year—especially mint, thyme, rosemary, and sage. All they need is sunshine and just a bit of care. Basil is an easy-to-grow tender annual herb.

1 Plant seeds 4 inches apart after the last frost, or transplant young basil plants into good garden soil, spacing the plants about 10 inches apart. Water well.

2 Pick basil throughout the summer, pinching off individual leaves or cutting the top few inches off the plant. Like all herbs, once the plant begins to flower the flavor in the leaves becomes less intense, so it works best to harvest the top leaves throughout the growing season.

3 In late summer you might want to let a few plants flower and go to seed. When the seed stalk has turned brown, clip it off and save the seeds to plant next year.

If you happen to end up with a bumper crop of basil, try making homemade Pesto (page 5).

Stove-Top Pizza

When asked about their favorite food, many children will tell you that they love, love, love pizza. Easy and fun to make, who cares if the pizzas are perfectly round? This pizza, made on top of the stove, is topped with chopped tomatoes, fresh basil, bell peppers, and a mix of mozzarella and Parmesan cheeses instead of traditional tomato sauce. You can also bake the pizzas in a very hot oven, at 450 to 500 degrees F.

Makes three 10-inch pizzas

Pizza Dough

 1 cup warm water

 ½ teaspoon baking yeast

 1 teaspoon honey

 ¾ cup whole wheat flour

 1¾ cups unbleached white flour

 ½ teaspoon baking powder

 ½ teaspoon salt

Pizza Toppings

 ¼ cup shredded Parmesan cheese

 ½ cup grated mozzarella cheese

 5 Roma tomatoes, diced

 ½ red bell pepper, diced

 2 tablespoons chopped fresh basil leaves

 ¼ teaspoon salt

 ⅛ teaspoon freshly ground black pepper

 2 teaspoons olive oil

What Kids Can Do

Almost everything!

Mix pizza dough

Grate cheese
(watch those knuckles)

Tear basil leaves

Roll out dough

Sprinkle toppings

Stove-Top Pizza *(continued)*

Cooks' Notes

✃ Serve with Tricolor Salad with Balsamic Vinaigrette (page 22).

✃ An outdoor grill works great when it's too hot in the kitchen. Grilled vegetables make good toppings, with or without tomatoes. Toss one or any combination of thickly sliced yellow or green squash, red onions with a drizzle of olive oil, minced fresh garlic, and a sprinkling of salt and pepper. Place directly on the hot grill and cook until lightly browned. Remove from the grill and let cool slightly. Cut or slice the vegetables into small pieces. Transfer the vegetables to the cooked side of the pizza dough, spreading them evenly.

✃ Grilled vegetables make an inviting side dish too. Just add a squeeze of lemon juice and a sprinkling of fresh parsley and basil.

1 Make the pizza dough: In a bowl, combine the warm water and yeast. Let sit for 2 to 3 minutes, until the yeast is dissolved. Stir in the honey and whole wheat flour. In a separate bowl, stir together the white flour, baking powder, and salt.

2 Add the dry ingredients to the whole wheat mixture, stirring to form a rough dough.

3 On a clean, lightly floured work surface, knead the dough for 1 to 2 minutes, until smooth. Cover the dough and let it rise while you prepare the pizza toppings.

4 Prepare the pizza toppings: In a small bowl, combine the cheeses. In another bowl, combine the tomatoes, bell peppers, basil, salt, pepper, and olive oil.

5 Divide the dough to make 3 equal balls. On a clean, lightly floured work surface, roll each ball into a circle that is 10 inches in diameter.

6 Cook the pizzas: Heat a 12-inch skillet or a large griddle over medium-high heat until it is hot. Transfer circle of dough onto the skillet or griddle and cook for 3 to 5 minutes. Flip the pizza crust.

7 Spread ⅓ of the tomato mixture over the crust. Top with ¼ cup of the cheese mixture. Cover the pizza and continue to cook until the toppings are hot and the bottom of the crust is golden brown, about 5 to 8 minutes. Remove the pizza to a cutting board and cut into wedges to serve. Repeat this process to make 2 more pizzas.

Did You Know?

According to popular legend, Pizza Margherita was first made in Naples, Italy, in 1889, in honor of the reigning queen of Italy. This pizza represented the colors of the Italian flag; red tomatoes, white cheese, and green basil. Pizzas became very popular in the United States when waves of Italian immigrants flooded the big cities of New York, Boston, and Chicago.

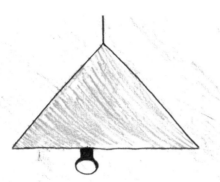

Draw a picture of the pizza you made today.
Write a sentence or two about your pizza.

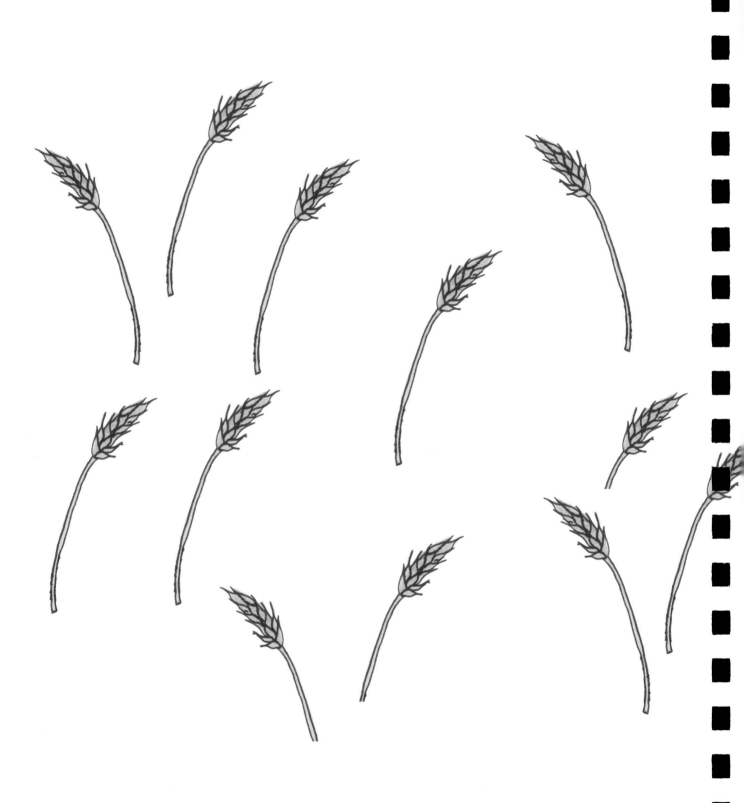

Stove-Top Breads

Stove-Top Breads

Ever since people discovered how to grind grain, breads have been cooked over fires around the globe. This has been going on for over 6,000 years. From India to the Americas, chapatis and tortillas are cooked and eaten every day, and most cultures have their own versions of flatbread. A dough or batter is easily made, and the breads cook quickly, using very little fuel.

Making any kind of bread is a magical way of involving kids in the kitchen. The process of measuring, mixing, kneading, and shaping or rolling dough just feels good! And eating fresh bread is like no other experience—soft and sweet, and a great way for kids to start eating and enjoying whole grains. From breadsticks to a quick injera from Ethiopia, these stove-top breads promise to make everyone comfortable with flour and a rolling pin. This chapter provides a quick introduction to easy breads made from wheat, teff, blue corn, or garbanzo flour, just a few of the many types of seeds and grains used across the world.

Corn Tortillas

What Kids Can Do

Everything!

Measure ingredients

Mix dough

Press tortillas

Cooks' Notes

✆ These tortillas are sturdy enough to use without frying, for making Black Bean Tostadas (page 48).

✆ They are also great for making soft tacos. Fill the tacos with grilled fish, crunchy lettuce, and thinly sliced radishes, then drizzle with Creamy Lime Dressing (page 25).

Children love working with dough. Kids enjoy squishing the dough to make tortillas using a tortilla press, but if you don't have one, see the note on the next page for alternative methods.

Makes 12 tortillas

2 cups masa harina de maíz

¼ teaspoon salt

1½ cups warm water

1 In a bowl, mix together the masa harina de maíz and salt. Add the water and mix with a wooden spoon or with your hands until a soft dough forms. Cover the dough with a clean cloth and let rest for 5 minutes.

2 Divide the dough into 12 equal pieces and roll each piece into a ball. To keep the dough from sticking to the tortilla press, put a square piece of plastic wrap (or parchment paper) on both surfaces of the press.

3 Put a ball of dough in the center of the plastic. Press the dough flat in the press. Pick up the tortilla with the plastic on both sides.

4 Peel off one piece of plastic and flip the tortilla off of the plastic onto a hot griddle. Cook for 1 to 2 minutes, until the underside of the tortilla is golden. Flip the tortilla and cook for 1 to 2 minutes more.

5 Continue the process until all of the dough has been made into tortillas. Stack the cooked tortillas on a plate and cover with a clean cloth. Serve warm.

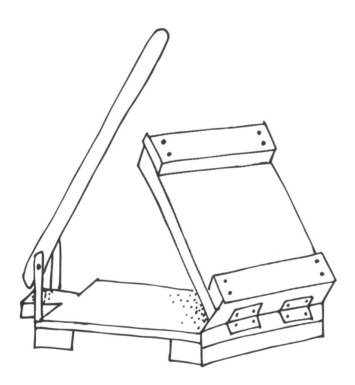

Cooks' Notes

If you don't have a tortilla press, one option is to use two cutting boards. Cover a cutting board with a piece of plastic wrap. Put a ball of dough on top of the plastic wrap, then cover the dough with another piece of plastic wrap. Place the second cutting board on top. Press on the top cutting board with both hands to flatten the dough. Slowly remove the top cutting board. Proceed as above, peeling the plastic wrap off one side of the tortilla and flipping onto a hot griddle to cook.

You can also form the tortillas in your hands: flatten the ball of dough, then pat it back and forth between your palms until it looks like a tortilla! This method will result in somewhat thicker tortillas that will take a bit more time to cook.

Blue Cornbread

What Kids Can Do

Measure ingredients

Crack egg

Mix batter

Cornbread is an American favorite. This Southwest version uses toasted blue cornmeal for an explosion of flavor, and it is best served warm just off the griddle or out of the oven. Kids will enjoy measuring and mixing the sky-blue batter.

Serves 4 to 6

> 1½ cups blue cornmeal
>
> ½ teaspoon baking soda
>
> ¼ teaspoon baking powder
>
> ½ teaspoon salt
>
> 1 large egg
>
> ¼ cup honey
>
> ¾ cup buttermilk
>
> ½ cup milk
>
> 2 tablespoons sunflower or other vegetable oil
>
> Additional oil for pan

1 In a bowl, mix together the cornmeal, baking soda, baking powder, and salt.

2 In another bowl, beat the egg and stir in the honey, buttermilk, milk, and oil.

3 Stir the wet ingredients into the dry ingredients and mix only until smooth.

4 Cook the cornbread using one of the methods below, and serve warm with butter or honey.

🌀 Stove-top method: Pour the batter into a well-oiled 9-inch cast-iron or nonstick sauté pan. Cover and cook over medium heat for 5 minutes. Reduce the heat to low and cook for about 10 more minutes, or until the top of the cornbread springs back when lightly touched. Serve warm.

🌀 Oven method: Preheat oven to 350 degrees F. Bake in a well-oiled 9-inch pan for 15 to 20 minutes, or until the top of the cornbread springs back.

Did You Know?

No one knows for sure exactly where in the Americas the first corn grew. But the oldest cultivated corn known today was found in the 1960s in a cave in central Mexico. There, archaeologists discovered tiny corncobs—each about a half inch long—from about 5,000 years ago. There are many varieties and colors of corn: white corn, yellow corn, red corn, and blue corn. Some types are best for drying or popping, and sweet corn is best to eat fresh. Old-fashioned heirloom varieties have rich flavor, and new super-sweet varieties taste almost like candy. When corn is grown together with beans and squash, they are known as the three sisters. Beans climb up the tall cornstalks, and squash plants take advantage of their shade.

Let's Grow Corn!

It's fun to have a cornfield, but you can grow corn if you have enough garden space for at least 16 plants so that they cross-pollinate and will make good-sized ears. Take the time to enjoy the tall corn—find a spot between the rows to sit quietly and just listen.

1 Plant at least 4 rows, 3 feet apart, in rich soil. Plant seeds outdoors when the soil has warmed, about 2 weeks after the last spring frost.

2 Make rows 3 feet apart, then plant the seeds 1 inch deep every 6 inches. Water well after planting and then every day or two until the seeds sprout.

3 When the plants are 4 inches tall, thin them so that the plants are spaced 12 inches apart. Keep watering and weed gently around the corn plants as they grow, as corn has shallow roots that you don't want to damage.

4 When the tassels begin to turn brown, the corn is ready to pick. To harvest, twist the ears off the cornstalk.

Mediterranean Flatbread

What Kids Can Do

Measure ingredients

Mix and knead dough

Chop or tear parsley

Cut and roll out flatbreads

Older kids can help cook
the flatbreads

Cooks' Note

For sesame flatbread, add
1 tablespoon of sesame
seeds to the dough, either
with or without the thyme
and parsley.

It's fun to experiment with the many kinds of flatbreads from around the world. The yogurt tenderizes the breads and the herbs brighten the flavor. These breads are meant to be eaten just off the griddle.

Makes 8 flatbreads

1½ cups warm water

1 teaspoon baking yeast

⅓ cup plain yogurt

2 tablespoons olive oil

1 teaspoon dried thyme leaves or 1 tablespoon fresh
thyme leaves

1 tablespoon chopped fresh parsley

¾ cup whole wheat flour

3 cups unbleached white flour

1 teaspoon baking powder

½ teaspoon salt

1 In a bowl, combine the water and yeast. Let sit for 2 minutes, until the yeast has dissolved. Stir in the yogurt, olive oil, thyme, parsley, and whole wheat flour.

2 In another bowl, mix together the white flour, baking powder, and salt. Gradually add the dry ingredients to the yeast mixture, stirring until a soft dough forms.

3 On a clean, lightly floured work surface, knead the dough for about 5 minutes, using a sprinkling of flour as necessary to prevent the dough from sticking. Shape the dough into a ball. Return the dough to the bowl, cover, and let the dough rise for 20 minutes. Note: If you have the time, let the dough rest for an hour or two for even fluffier flatbreads.

4 Divide the dough into 8 equal pieces. Form each piece of dough into a ball. Use a rolling pin to roll each piece of dough into a circle 5 to 6 inches in diameter and about ¼ inch thick.

5 Cook the flatbreads on a hot griddle for 2 to 3 minutes on each side, until golden brown and slightly puffed. Stack the cooked flatbreads on a plate and cover with a clean cloth. Serve warm.

Breadsticks

What Kids Can Do

Almost everything!

Measure ingredients

Mix and knead dough

Roll out breadsticks

Brush the breadsticks with olive oil and sprinkle with salt

Older kids can help cook the breadsticks

It is believed that breadsticks might have first been made during medieval times. But they were almost certainly made popular by bakers in northern Italy in the late 1600s. The Italian word for breadsticks is *grissini*. They are long, thin, and crisp—perfect for dipping.

Makes 32 breadsticks

> 1¼ cups warm water
>
> 2 teaspoons baking yeast
>
> 2 tablespoons olive oil
>
> 1 tablespoon honey
>
> 1 teaspoon dried rosemary or ½ teaspoon cracked black peppercorns
>
> 1½ teaspoons salt
>
> 1 cup whole wheat flour
>
> 2½ cups white flour
>
> Additional olive oil and coarse or kosher salt

1 In a bowl, combine the water and yeast. Let sit for 2 minutes, until the yeast is dissolved. Add the olive oil, honey, rosemary or peppercorns, salt, and whole wheat flour, stirring well.

2 Add the white flour, 1 cup at a time, stirring until a stiff dough forms. On a clean, lightly floured work surface knead the dough for 3 to 5 minutes, until smooth.

3 Divide the dough into 8 equal pieces. Form each piece into a circle about 3 inches in diameter. Now divide each piece into 4 equal pieces. There will be a total of 32 pieces. Roll each piece of dough into a cylinder about 8 inches long and place on baking sheet.

4 Cook the breadsticks on a hot griddle, brushing with olive oil and sprinkling with salt as they cook. Use tongs to turn them as they brown. Let the breadsticks cool before serving.

Cooks' Notes

Vary the flavors:

- Use both peppercorns and dried or fresh rosemary.
- Use 1 tablespoon chopped fresh garlic.
- Add 2 to 3 tablespoons grated Parmesan cheese to the wet ingredients.

These breadsticks can also be baked in the oven, but we prefer the rustic, unevenly browned look of the stove-top method. To bake, preheat oven to 425 degrees F. Bake the breadsticks on a lightly oiled baking sheet for about 15 to 18 minutes, turning at least once during the baking, until lightly browned and almost crisp.

Let's Grow Wheat!

Growing a little patch of wheat in your backyard garden is one way to give children a glimpse of the beauty of golden waving wheat—and then you get to harvest it! It is fun to grind the precious seeds, called wheat berries, into flour for baking, or crack them to cook as a hearty breakfast cereal, or just save the beautiful stalks.

Winter wheat is planted in the fall, and spring wheat in the early spring.

1 Find out which types grow best in your area, then cultivate good soil so that it is weed free.

2 Scatter the wheat seeds about 1 inch apart. A fun way to plant wheat is to give children handfuls of seed and tell them to spin around slowly, sprinkling the seeds over the ground as they turn. If you see a few bare spots, fill them in with more seed, then gently rake in the seeds to cover them with soil.

3 Tamp the seed by walking over the planted area, then water well.

4 Water every day until the seeds sprout. The young plants look like blades of grass when they are small, but they will grow to about 3 feet tall.

5 When the stalks turn from green to golden, harvest with a scythe or hedge clippers. Thresh the wheat to remove the seeds from the stalks in a wheelbarrow, beating the wheat with a heavy stick.

6 To separate the wheat from the chaff (the papery seed covering), use a basket to toss the wheat into the air on a day when the wind is gently blowing—or use a fan on low. It's an experiment!

Label the parts of the wheat plant.
Draw a line from the name of the plant part to the part of the plant in the drawing.

Leaf

Root

Stem

Wheat Berries

Socca

What Kids Can Do

Measure ingredients

Mix batter

Older kids can help
ladle the batter and
cook the breads

Cooks' Note

Garbanzo flour (also known
as chickpea flour) can be
purchased in natural-food
stores or specialty grocery
stores.

Socca is a street-food specialty in southern France, especially on the
Mediterranean coast in the city of Nice, where it is served right off
the hot pan and wrapped in a paper cone. It is tasty on its own as a
snack, or it can be used as a wrap for spring greens and crumbled
feta or your favorite goat cheese.

Makes seven 7-inch breads

1 cup garbanzo flour

½ teaspoon salt

½ teaspoon baking soda

¼ teaspoon ground cumin (optional)

1¼ cups water

2 teaspoons olive oil

Additional olive oil for cooking

Freshly ground black pepper and coarse salt

1 In a bowl, mix together the flour, salt, and cumin (if using). Slowly whisk in the water and olive oil to form a smooth batter. Let the batter rest for 1 to 2 hours, covered, at room temperature.

2 Heat a griddle or crepe pan over high heat. Drizzle with olive oil, and ladle ¼ cup of batter onto the griddle or into the pan, spreading the batter evenly to form round, thin, pancake-like breads. When the top of the socca appears set and the underside is lightly browned, use a spatula to turn it over to finish cooking, 2 to 3 minutes on each side.

3 Flip the socca onto a cutting board. Sprinkle it with pepper and coarse salt.

4 Repeat this process to cook the remaining socca, adding a small amount of oil each time. Serve the socca warm, either whole or sliced into wedges.

Injera

What Kids Can Do

Measure ingredients

Mix batter

Older kids can help cook the injera

Cooks' Notes

- Serve with Ethiopian Lentils with Tikil Gomen (page 74).

- Teff flour can be purchased in natural-food stores or specialty grocery stores. If you like to experiment, millet flour can be substituted for teff in this recipe.

Did You Know?

Teff is a type of millet, an underrated grain that Americans mostly use as birdseed. Millet has a golden sweetness when cooked as hot breakfast cereal or ground into flour and mixed into bread or pancakes.

Ethiopian flatbread is made from teff, a tiny, nutritious grain. Traditionally, a fermented batter is cooked into large, thin pancakes, then served as an edible plate with lentils, meat, or vegetables arranged on top. Kids enjoy the challenge of using pieces of injera to scoop up food instead of eating with a fork or spoon! This quick recipe works best when the batter is cooked on a cast-iron griddle.

Makes fifteen 6-inch breads

> **1½ cups teff flour**
>
> **¾ cup unbleached white flour**
>
> **¾ teaspoon baking soda**
>
> **½ teaspoon salt**
>
> **¼ cup plain yogurt**
>
> **3 cups water**
>
> **3 tablespoons butter, for cooking**

1 In a bowl, combine the teff flour, unbleached white flour, baking soda, and salt.

2 Gradually add the water and yogurt, whisking to form a smooth batter.

3 Heat a griddle over medium-high heat. When hot, add a small amount of butter. As soon as the butter has melted, ladle ¼ cup of batter onto the hot griddle, spreading the batter evenly to form round, thin, pancake-like breads.

4 Cook until bubbles form on top and the batter appears set, about 2 minutes. Turn the injera and cook about 1 minute more. Stack the cooked injera on a plate and cover with a clean cloth. Serve warm.

Chapatis

Indian cuisine includes many, many kinds of flatbreads. For tender chapatis, it's important to make a soft dough, let it rest, then cook the chapatis quickly over high heat. Kids love to eat them hot off the griddle.

Makes sixteen 4-inch breads

3 cups unbleached white flour

1 cup whole wheat flour

1 teaspoon salt

¼ cup butter, melted

1½ cups warm water

1 In a bowl, mix together the unbleached white flour, whole wheat flour, and salt. Stir in the melted butter. Add the water gradually, mixing until a soft dough is formed.

2 On a lightly floured, clean work surface, knead the dough for about 5 minutes. Shape the dough into a ball and return it to the bowl. Cover with a clean cloth and let rest for at least 30 minutes or up to 4 hours.

3 Divide the dough into 16 equal pieces. Form each piece into a ball. Use a rolling pin to roll out each ball of dough into a circle that is about 4 inches in diameter.

4 Cook the chapatis on a hot griddle for 2 to 3 minutes on each side, until lightly browned and slightly puffed. Stack the cooked chapatis on a plate and cover with a clean cloth. Serve warm.

What Kids Can Do

Measure ingredients

Mix dough

Roll out chapatis

Cooks' Notes

Use these little breads to scoop up Red Lentils with Carrot Rice Pilaf and Cucumber Raita (page 70).

For a special treat, put ½ teaspoon of butter inside each ball of dough before rolling out the chapatis.

Cinnamon Flatbread

What Kids Can Do

Measure ingredients

Mix dough

Roll out flatbreads

Older kids can help
cook the flatbreads

Everyone loves cinnamon toast. This slightly sweet flatbread makes a scrumptious after-school snack.

Makes sixteen 4-inch flatbreads

2 cups warm water

2 teaspoons baking yeast

½ cup plain yogurt

3 tablespoons honey or sugar

2 cups whole wheat flour

3½ cups unbleached white flour

1 teaspoon baking powder

½ teaspoon salt

¼ teaspoon cinnamon

2 teaspoons olive oil

Additional flour for kneading

1 In a bowl, combine the water and yeast. Let sit for two minutes, until the yeast dissolves. Add the yogurt, honey, and whole wheat flour and stir until well mixed. Gradually add the unbleached white flour along with the baking powder, salt, and cinnamon, mixing to form a soft dough.

2 Turn the dough out onto a lightly floured work surface and knead for 3 to 5 minutes. Add only enough flour to prevent the dough from sticking. Rub the dough with the olive oil and let rest for 30 minutes to 1 hour.

3 Divide the dough into 16 equal pieces. Use a rolling pin to roll each piece of dough into a circle about 4 inches in diameter and ⅛ inch thick.

4 Cook the flatbreads on a hot griddle for 2 to 3 minutes on each side, until lightly browned and slightly puffed. Stack the flatbreads on a plate and cover with a clean cloth. Serve warm.

Close your eyes and remember a happy time in your life that includes food.
Draw a picture of your memory, then write a sentence or two
that describes how you felt.

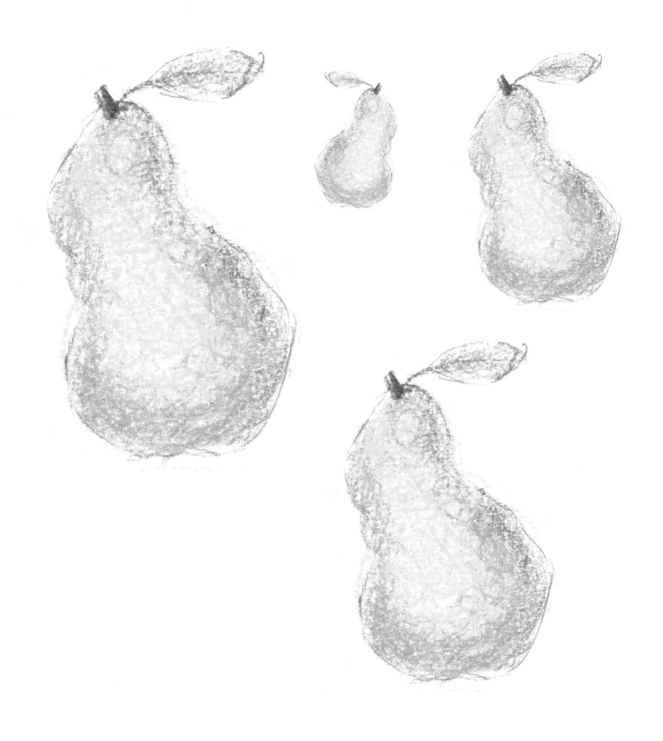

Fruits and Sweets

Fruits and Sweets

Fruits are nature's sweet jewels. If you are lucky enough to have a fruit tree in your backyard or an orchard nearby, picking (and eating) juicy-ripe fruit may be a seasonal delight for your family. These days, depending on where you live, farmers' markets offer locally grown fruits at their peak: strawberries in late spring; then cherries, apricots, peaches, plums, and figs in summer; melons, blackberries, red and golden raspberries, and blueberries, followed by tart-sweet grapes, apples, pears, and quince in the fall. In warm climates, citrus fruits bear in winter, including tiny kumquats, with their sweet peels and sour centers.

Tasting different types of fruits from the same family is one way for children, and adults, to learn about their own personal preferences—and to observe how tastes may change over time. Different varieties of the same fruit often present varied flavors and textures, with some sweeter, some more tart, some soft, crisp, chewy, or crunchy.

Perfectly ripe summer fruits like apricots and peaches are a treat on their own, or dressed up just a little with a dollop of whipped cream. This chapter focuses on simple fruit recipes, along with a few other favorite desserts: cookies, crepes, and slightly sweet coconut rice balls.

You might also make walnut-stuffed dates or put out a little bowl of nuts, dried fruit, and chocolate chips for a sweet finish or afternoon treat.

Golden Fruits

What Kids Can Do

Wash fruits

Peel oranges

Peel bananas

Squeeze lime juice

Coconut and freshly squeezed lime juice take this fruit salad up a notch. Enjoy it as a snack or for a refreshing finish to a meal.

Serves 4

2 bananas, peeled and sliced

1 ripe mango, peeled and cut into ½-inch pieces

2 oranges, peeled and cut into ¾-inch pieces

2 tablespoons unsweetened shredded or shaved coconut

2 tablespoons fresh lime juice

1 In a bowl, combine all the ingredients and stir lightly. Serve immediately.

Note: If you want to make it ahead of time, put everything together but the bananas, then add the sliced bananas just before serving.

Rainforest Macaroons

These cookies can be whipped up in a flash and are a favorite to make and to eat. They combine the richness of coconut and chocolate in a light meringue. Kids are fascinated by the transformation of clear gelatinous egg whites into a fluffy cloud that looks like whipped cream. They can take turns beating egg whites with a hand-powered egg beater. Folding is an art that most school-age children can master when guided by a quick demonstration and a reminder to "be gentle."

Makes about 2 dozen cookies

> 2 egg whites, at room temperature
>
> Pinch salt
>
> ⅓ cup sugar
>
> 2 cups unsweetened shredded coconut
>
> ½ cup semisweet chocolate chips

1 Preheat oven to 325 degrees F. Oil 2 cookie sheets or line with baking parchment.

2 Beat the egg whites and salt until frothy. Gradually add the sugar, continuing to beat just until the mixture forms stiff peaks. Gently fold in the coconut and chocolate chips.

3 Drop by rounded teaspoonfuls onto the prepared cookie sheets. Bake for about 10 minutes, until light golden. Let cool for 5 minutes on the cookie sheets and then remove the cookies to a cooling rack.

What Kids Can Do

Measure ingredients

Fold in coconut and chocolate chips

Spoon batter onto cookie sheets

Tangy Melon

What Kids Can Do

Scrape out melon seeds

Scoop melon balls

Squeeze lime juice

Tear or chop mint leaves

We know that kids adore melon—the juiciness, the sweetness, the messiness. Add a splash of lime juice and you've got just the right way to serve melon for breakfast, as a snack, or for dessert.

Serves 4 to 6

1 cantaloupe, honeydew, or other melon

Juice of 1 lime

3 to 5 fresh mint leaves, chopped (optional)

1 Cut the melon in half. Use a spoon to scrape the seeds out of the melon. Use a melon scoop to make melon balls. Put the melon balls in a bowl.

2 Stir in the lime juice and chopped mint leaves, if using. Serve immediately.

Let's Grow Melons!

Melons are one of summer's sweet pleasures. The plants like warm weather, so plant the seeds after the last frost of the spring.

1   Plant melon seeds 1 inch deep and spaced 1 foot apart in rich soil.

2   Water every day until the seeds sprout. Thin the young plants so that they are spaced 2 to 3 feet apart in all directions.

3   Pull the weeds out of your melon patch, and in 75 to 95 days, depending on the variety of melon, you'll be ready to pick ripe melons. You can often tell when a cantaloupe is ripe by its sweet fragrance.

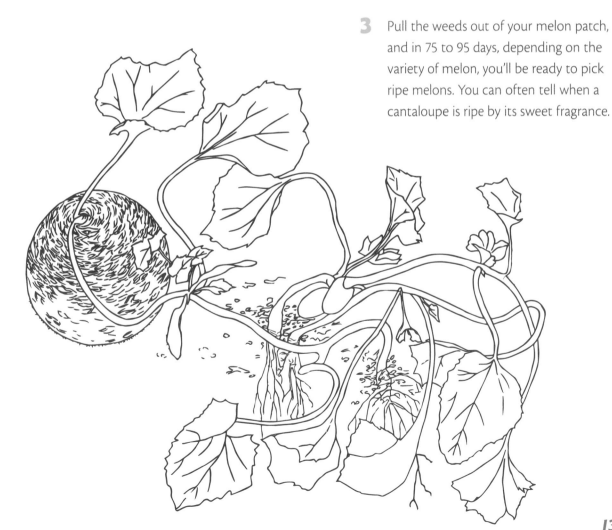

Fruit Jewels

The cut sides of the fruits in this salad look like shining jewels.

Serves 4 to 6

2 cups black or red grapes, halved

3 kiwi fruits, peeled, halved, and sliced

2 oranges, peeled, quartered, and sliced

Juice of 1 lime

1 Combine all the ingredients in a serving bowl. Stir gently and serve immediately.

What Kids Can Do

Wash fruits

Take grapes off stems

Peel oranges

Slice kiwi

Squeeze lime juice

Oranges with Fresh Mint

Oranges and mint may not seem to go together, but the combination is a hit with both children and adults. When they are in season, use a variety of citrus such as Cara Cara oranges, blood oranges, or tangerines, and enjoy comparing the different flavors and colors.

Serves 4 to 6

6 oranges

¼ cup chopped fresh mint leaves

1 Peel and section the oranges. Cut each orange section into about 3 pieces and put into a serving bowl.

2 Add the chopped mint leaves and stir gently to combine. Serve immediately.

Homemade Applesauce

Making applesauce yourself is fast, cheap, and much tastier than the store-bought kind. Use a handy apple corer to cut the apples into slices, and then even little kids can cut the slices into small pieces using butter knives. The smaller the pieces, the faster the sauce will cook!

Makes about 3 cups—it depends on the size of the apples!

6 apples (about 8 cups apple pieces)

1 cup water

¼ cup honey or sugar (optional)

½ teaspoon cinnamon (optional)

1 Use an apple cutter to core and cut the apples into wedges. Cut each wedge into 4 pieces. Combine the apple pieces and water in a saucepan.

2 Cook the apples over medium heat, covered, for about 25 minutes, until the apples are tender and cooked through.

3 Stir in honey or sugar and cinnamon, if using, and cook for 5 minutes more. Remove from the heat.

What Kids Can Do

Wash apples

Cut apples into pieces

Let's Grow Apples!

There is nothing like picking ripe fruit right from the tree! If you plant a young apple tree when you are seven years old, by the time you are ten or eleven you may be lucky enough to taste a few juicy apples from your tree. And—if you care for the tree well by watering it deeply and adding compost to the ground in an area 4 to 5 feet around the tree—by the time you are thirteen there will likely be enough fruit from that one tree to share with your family and friends!

Dried Apple Rings

Dried apples make a satisfying snack. Like raisins, dried apples are sweet and nutritious. Use both green and red apples for a colorful mix.

6 to 8 apples

1 Use an apple corer to remove the apple cores. Slice the apples into ⅛-inch-thick rings.

2 String the apples onto a string and hang it in a warm room to dry. Make sure the apple slices are not touching each other, so that they will dry evenly.

3 Let the apples hang for at least 3 to 6 days, until they become leathery and dry. Store in ziplock plastic bags in a cool place or in the freezer.

What Kids Can Do

Wash apples

Core apples

Hang apple slices on string

Pack dried apples into bags

Cooks' Note

An apple peeler and slicer that clamps to a table is a fun kitchen gadget—it cuts an apple into a thin spiral.

Use your best penmanship to write the names of these apples in alphabetical order: Jonagold, Rome, Beacon, Tolman Sweet, Cortland, Melba, Fameuse, Golden Delicious, Lodi, Northern Spy, Crispin, Yellow Transparent, McIntosh, Lobo Amélioré, Wealthy, Idared, Royal Red Delicious, Jonamac, Paula Red, Liberty, Tydeman's Early Worcester, Cox's Orange Pippin, Honey Crisp, Braeburn, Pink Lady.

Baked Pears

Baked pears are an easy-to-make and adaptable dessert. This is also a good way to use pears when their flavor or sweetness isn't quite perfect.

Serves 4 to 6

3 ripe pears

2 tablespoons brown sugar

⅛ teaspoon ground cinnamon

¼ cup water

1 Preheat the oven to 350 degrees F. Cut the pears lengthwise in half. Scoop out the cores and seeds. Place cut pears cut-side up in a pie plate or small baking dish.

2 In a small bowl, combine the brown sugar and cinnamon. Spoon the mixture into the hollows of the pears, dividing evenly. Pour the water into the bottom of the baking dish.

3 Bake the pears for about 25 minutes, or until tender. Serve warm.

What Kids Can Do

Wash pears

Spoon filling into the hollows of the pears

Cooks' Note

Add a handful of fresh or frozen raspberries or blackberries or a sprinkling of nuts and raisins on top of the pears in the baking dish before baking.

Did You Know?

Pears are one of the few fruits best picked before they are ripe. If they are left on the tree until they turn yellow, the natural sugars turn to starch crystals and the pear will taste gritty. It is fine to buy pears at the grocery store when they are still hard—just let them sit at room temperature for several days. You can tell when the fruit is ripe by gently pressing the top of the pear. When it is just a little bit softer than the rest of the pear, the pear is ready to eat!

Strawberry Crepes

What Kids Can Do

Measure flour

Crack eggs

Mix crepe batter

Wash and slice berries

Cooks' Note

✂ Whole wheat pastry flour can be purchased in natural-food stores or specialty grocery stores.

Crepes often seem like an exotic mystery. In fact, these thin French pancakes are easy to make—a treat for breakfast, an afternoon snack, or dessert. They require just a bit of patience since you have to cook them one at a time!

Makes about ten 7-inch crepes

Crepes

2 eggs

1 cup milk

Zest of ½ orange or lemon

¼ cup whole wheat pastry flour

⅓ cup sifted unbleached white flour

1 teaspoon sugar

⅛ teaspoon salt

1 tablespoon butter, melted

Additional butter for cooking

1 In a bowl, whisk together the whole wheat pastry flour, white flour, sugar, and salt.

2 In a separate bowl, whisk the eggs until frothy. Add the milk and orange zest and whisk until smooth.

3 Add the wet ingredients to the dry ingredients, whisking constantly until smooth. Stir in the melted butter and whisk again.

4 Ladle the crepe batter into a liquid measuring cup or pitcher. Heat a 6- or 7-inch cast-iron skillet or nonstick pan over high heat. Melt a small amount of butter to coat the bottom and sides of the pan. Pour 3 to 4 tablespoons of batter into the pan and immediately swirl the pan around to distribute the batter evenly. Cook for 1 to 2 minutes, until the bottom is golden. Flip the crepe and cook for 1 minute more on the second side. Remove to a plate. Cook the rest of the crepes, adding a little butter to the pan as needed.

5 Spoon berries and a little whipped cream into the center of each crepe. Fold in half. Garnish with a dollop of whipped cream and a few more berries.

Strawberries

6 cups strawberries
1 to 2 tablespoons sugar
¼ cup orange juice

1 Slice the strawberries and put them into a bowl. Sprinkle with sugar and stir in the orange juice. Let sit for at least 15 minutes before serving. This helps the strawberries to become juicy. If the berries need more juice, add a little more orange juice.

Whipped Cream

Makes about 2 cups

Cooks' Note

If the weather is hot, chill the bowl and the beaters in the freezer before whipping the cream. Otherwise, the cream may turn to butter!

1 cup heavy cream

2 teaspoons sugar

¼ teaspoon vanilla extract

1 Combine the cream, sugar, and vanilla in a bowl. Whip with an electric mixer until soft peaks form. Serve immediately.

Note: Whip the cream by hand with a whisk in a chilled bowl. It builds muscles!

Coconut Rice Balls

One of our most beloved recipes, the combination of soft sushi rice and coconut milk with a hint of almond flavor and a pretty mango garnish transforms these simple ingredients into a fancy dessert.

Makes about fifteen 1-inch rice balls

½ cup sushi rice

1 cup water

Pinch salt

¼ cup coconut milk

2 tablespoons sugar

⅛ teaspoon pure almond extract

½ cup shredded coconut

¼ cup mango slivers

What Kids Can Do

Wash rice

Measure ingredients

Roll rice balls

Decorate rice balls with slivers of mango

1 Combine the rice, water, and salt in a small saucepan. Bring to a boil over high heat. Reduce heat to medium and partially cover. Cook until all of the water is absorbed, about 25 minutes. Remove from the heat.

2 Stir the coconut milk, sugar, and almond extract into the rice. Let cool to lukewarm.

3 Using wet fingers, take about 1 teaspoon of rice and roll it into a ball. Roll each rice ball in coconut to coat it.

4 Cut the mango pieces into thin strips, ¼ inch wide and 1 inch long. Just before serving, garnish each rice ball with a sliver of mango.

Mango Fool

What Kids Can Do

Measure ingredients

Help fold whipped cream into mango puree

Cooks' Note

The mango pit is a sweet treat—enjoy the messiness!

A fool is an English dessert that traditionally combines cooked fruit with custard. This sunrise-colored version is best eaten the same day it is made.

Serves 5

3 large, ripe mangoes

½ cup heavy cream

3 tablespoons sugar or maple syrup

¼ teaspoon almond extract (optional)

1 Peel and pit the mangoes.

2 Puree the mango pieces using a blender or food processor. Strain the pureed pulp through a sieve into a bowl.

3 In a bowl, combine the cream, sugar or maple syrup, and almond extract, if using. Whip with electric mixer to medium peaks.

4 Gently fold the whipped cream into the mango puree. Ladle the mixture into dessert cups and refrigerate until ready to serve.

Cooking Words

boil: To heat a liquid until bubbles break the surface (212°F for water at sea level). Boil also means to cook food in a boiling liquid.

colander: A bowl with a pattern of small holes on the sides and bottom that allows liquids to drain through, while the solids remain inside the sieve itself. Colanders are usually made of stainless steel, enameled steel, or plastic.

core: To remove the inner part of a fruit that contains the seeds, such as the core of an apple.

dice: To cut into small cubes.

dissolve: To incorporate a dry ingredient into a liquid, so that no grains of the dry ingredient can be seen or felt.

drain: To pour off liquid gradually or completely.

garnish: A decorative, edible accompaniment to a finished dish. Garnishes can be placed under, around, or on food. They vary from simple sprigs of parsley to exotically carved vegetables. Garnishes should be appealing to the eye and complement the flavors of the dish.

grate: To shred a large piece of food into smaller long, thin strips.

griddle: A flat pan that is used to cook foods like pancakes, with a minimal amount of fat or oil. Griddles are usually made of thick, heavy metals such as cast iron.

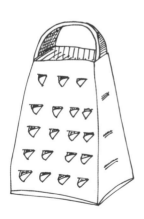

ingredient: Something that forms part of a mixture. In cooking, a recipe tells which ingredients are used to prepare a dish.

knead: A technique used to mix and work dough in order to form it into a pliable mass. By hand, kneading is done with a pressing-folding-turning action.

kosher salt: A large grained salt that contains no iodine or other additives. The word "kosher" comes from the Hebrew language and means "proper" or "pure." Kosher food has been prepared under the supervision of a rabbi (a Jewish religious leader).

matchsticks: The shape of food that has been cut into thin pieces, about the size of wooden matchsticks. Most commonly, matchsticks are cut from firm vegetables like carrots.

mince: To chop or cut food into very small pieces.

mortar and pestle: A mortar is a very hard bowl, and a pestle is a rounded, bat-like instrument. As a pair, the mortar and pestle are used for grinding and pulverizing spices, herbs, and other foods.

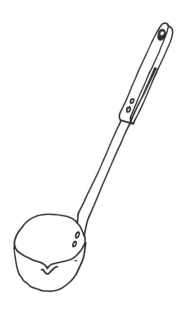

sauté: To cook quickly in a small amount of fat or oil.

simmer: To cook gently in a liquid at a temperature just below the boiling point.

slice: To cut into thin pieces.

steam: To cook food by placing it above (not directly in) boiling water, allowing the heat and moisture of the steam to cook the food.

whisk: A kitchen tool with strands of looped wire used for whipping air into eggs or other ingredients. To whisk means to mix or beat with a wire whisk.

zest: To grate the colored outer peel of citrus fruits. Do not grate the white part of the peel, as it has a bitter taste.

Illustrations

Children's Drawings

Line Drawings

Photographs

Acknowledgments

Sometimes we don't notice when a dream is coming true. In the case of this cookbook, however, gifts, talents, and generosity came from more people than we can mention, all with such exuberance along the way.

First and foremost, to cookbook author Cheryl Alters Jamison, mentor-extraordinaire, friend, and one we lean on, thank you for taking us on this journey—and thank you also to both Cheryl and Deborah Madison, for blessing us with a foreword that makes us blush. To Gabbie Gonzales, who brought her promise, youthful energy, undying good humor, and heart—thank you for making this book happen with your belief in and love for Cooking with Kids. Thank you to Stephanie Morris for creating exquisite drawings on demand year after year and for combining your artistic talents with your love of food, children, and education. And thanks also to the Cooking with Kids staff over these many years, too numerous to name, but especially Linda Apodaca and Deborah Barbe, who have each dedicated over fifteen years to our work together. Without all of you so many of these recipes would not exist, and we are grateful for your commitment and devotion to all the sticky fingers, loud voices, and silly questions in every cooking class you taught—plus all the dish towels you laundered! Thank you to Rachel Shreve for stepping up again and again with hard work, precision, and blossoming creativity—plus for your brilliant design sense, skills, and for shopping and testing recipes. Thank you also to Lily Hofstra, who patiently proofread the text over and over again, offering great ideas and kindly suggesting clarifications, and to Anna Farrier, whose clear-eyed view advanced the process. A hearty and heartfelt thank-you with hugs to the Cooking with Kids Board of Directors, who have nurtured and guided us through their vision, generosity, and commitment. Finally, we lovingly dedicate this cookbook to the children, families, and teachers of Santa Fe, New Mexico, who inspire us every day.

Index